MICROSOFT WINDOWS 8®

FEATURING THE WINDOWS 8.1 UPDATE

MADE EASY

This is a **FLAME TREE** book
First published 2014

Publisher and Creative Director: Nick Wells
Project Editor: Polly Prior
Art Director and Layout Design: Mike Spender
Digital Design and Production: Chris Herbert
Screenshots: James Stables
Copy Editor: Anna Groves
Technical Editor: Mark Mayne
Proofreader: Dawn Laker
Indexer: Helen Snaith

Special Thanks: Esme Chapman, Matt Knight and Catherine Taylor

This edition first published 2014 by
FLAME TREE PUBLISHING
Crabtree Hall, Crabtree Lane
Fulham, London SW6 6TY
United Kingdom

www.flametreepublishing.com

14 16 18 17 15
1 3 5 7 9 10 8 6 4 2

© 2014 Flame Tree Publishing

ISBN 978-1-78361-233-8

A CIP record for this book is available from the British Library upon request.

Printed in China

All non-screenshot pictures are courtesy of Shutterstock and © the following photographers: Piotr Adamowicz: 88; Ermolaev Alexander: 155, 235, 240; alphaspirit: 6, 178; Ammentorp Photography: 137; Andresr: 131; asharkyu: 6, 144; baranq: 38; Peter Bernik: 215; Ana Blazic Pavlovic: 30; Blend Images: 11; bikeriderlondon: 43, 97, 166; cunaplus: 223; Diego Cervo: 120; Ditty_about_summer: 197; Dean Drobot: 146; EDHAR: 12; Elnur: 107; Four Oaks: 5, 62; Goodluz: 13; Hasloo Group Production Studio: 109; indigolotos: 18; Julia Ivantsova: 85; EM Karuna: 90; Khosro: 201; krichie: 147; l i g h t p o e t: 234; Oleksiy Mark: 5, 110; michaeljung: 35; Minerva Studio: 227; nmedia: 49; Sergey Novikov: 101; oliveromg: 183; ollyy: 7, 108, 216; Tyler Olson: 77; Edyta Pawlowska: 52; Pressmaster: 194; prochasson frederic: 121; puhhha: 141; racorn: 169, 187; ruigsantos: 80; Lisa S.: 8; Valery Sidelnykov: 190; Nikola Solev: 104; StockLite: 10, 86, 231; szefei: 159; Jeff Thrower: 199; Denis Vrublevski: 50; wavebreakmedia: 73; Yeko Photo Studio: 3; Jurgen Ziewe: 4, 14

All product image shots courtesy of and ©: Acer Inc.: 10; ASUSTeK Computer Inc.: 30; Buffalo Americas, Inc.: 149; Canon (UK) Ltd 2014: 83, 246; Dell: 28, 31; Hewlett-Packard Development Company, L.P.: 29; IBM: 16; Intel Corporation: 25, 249; LG Electronics.: 26; Lenovo: 1, 27, 45, 209; Microsoft: 21, 22, 23 (both); Misco UK Limited: 102; NETGEAR®: 152; Nokia: 148; Samsung: 25 (b), 31; Sony Electronics Inc.: 17; Toshiba Europe GmbH: 28, 249; Western Digital Technologies, Inc: 248

MICROSOFT WINDOWS 8®

FEATURING THE WINDOWS 8.1 UPDATE

MADE EASY

JAMES STABLES

FLAME TREE
PUBLISHING

CONTENTS

Introducing the basics of the operating system, this chapter is designed to give you an overview of why Windows 8.1 exists, and provide you with inspiration for getting more out of the operating system. Here you'll find new ideas for ways to use your Windows 8.1 PC and an at-a-glance guide to the new interface.

GETTING STARTED **62**

This chapter tells you everything you need to know to start using Windows 8.1. From getting installed and set up for the first time, to adding essential security, backing up and giving your PC its own personal look and feel, this chapter walks any new user through their first hour with Windows 8.1.

ALL ABOUT APPS. **110**

One of the biggest improvements brought by Windows 8.1 compared to previous generations of the OS is apps. This chapter explains everything you need to know about apps in Windows 8.1, from how to use the stock offerings to advice on buying and downloading new apps from the Windows Store.

GETTING CONNECTED.....................144

Whether you're connecting your PC to the Internet for the first time, or looking to get into advanced networking, this chapter deals with turning your PC from a solitary bunch of wires into an ever-connected portal to a world of information. We'll teach you how to get started using the web safely and how to connect your household's PCs together, as well as how to reap the benefits of the latest advances in cloud computing.

MUSIC, VIDEO & PHOTOS.................178

Windows 8.1 isn't just about speeding up your PC, getting it working well and maintaining your files. It's about having fun and doing what you love. We have in-depth guides to the new Xbox Music and Xbox Video apps, which enable on-demand access to a world of tunes and film, as well as the powerful Windows Media Player app, which you can use for ripping CDs, syncing to mobile devices and managing libraries. There's also a complete guide to the Pictures app, which is great for editing and enjoying pictures on your PC.

TROUBLESHOOTING & MAINTENANCE 216

Running into problems is one of the things that people fear most about technology, which is why we've devoted an entire chapter to dealing with bugs in the system. Everyone runs into problems from time to time, so this chapter arms you with everything you need to know. Of course, PC problems are less likely to arise on a well-maintained system, so we explain how to use the plethora of tools built into Windows to keep things running smoothly. From saving space to keeping your disks in optimum working order, this guide tells you everything you need to know about keeping Windows 8.1 in tiptop condition.

INTRODUCTION

Starting out with a new PC can be difficult, especially if you're a new user who's unfamiliar with the fast-paced world of technology. Luckily, this guide tells you everything you need to know to get started with Windows 8.1. From the very basics to expert tools, *Windows 8 Made Easy* has it all. The following pages explain how to use this in-depth guide.

Above: Don't despair! This book will help you get the most out of Windows 8.1.

YOUR ESSENTIAL KEEPSAKE

Windows 8 Made Easy isn't just a one-off guide to the basics of the operating system; it's your companion for every aspect of computing. It's designed to be a long-term reference tool, an essential companion which can be turned to whenever you need some guidance. The clear chapters and at-a-glance index means you can return to it at anytime, and the troubleshooting guide in Chapter 6 will help you solve nearly every Windows problem, whenever it arises.

WINDOWS 8 OR WINDOWS 8.1?

As we outline on page 16, Windows 8.1 is the 2013 update to Microsoft's Windows 8, which was released in 2012. This book has been written specifically for the Home version of Windows 8.1 and covers all the new features that the update has brought with it. If you are running Windows 8, or even Windows 7, don't fear, you can still use this guide; even better, if you turn to page 19, we will show you how to upgrade to 8.1, for free.

CLEAR SCREENSHOTS

We've spent time taking stills of every aspect of the operating system, and we've tested and demonstrated every guide and taken screenshots along the way. They're not just there for decoration; they're designed for you to see where the options are and how to get to them, making the guides easy to follow and to help you really start getting to grips with this brilliant operating system.

Above: All the screenshots in this book have been chosen to highlight or further illustrate what is being said in the text.

EXPERT ADVICE

Windows 8 Made Easy is the result of nearly ten years of experience writing guides and tutorials about the Windows operating system. The author's wealth of experience of writing and editing magazines, books, periodicals and even instructional videos on Windows XP, Vista, 7 and, more recently, Windows 8, means this guide is the only resource you'll need.

DESIGNED FOR EVERYONE

Not only is *Windows 8 Made Easy* designed for every type of user – beginner to advanced – it also covers every type of device. Windows 8.1 isn't just designed for mouse and keyboard users; it has opened up entire new categories of PC. From hybrids to touch-screen Ultrabooks, tablets and all-in-ones, PCs have changed completely in the last few years. This guide embraces those changes and we've incorporated instructions, depending on whether you're using the tried-and-tested mouse or a brand new touch screen. What's more, Chapter 2 has special gestures for every type of user, so everyone can get the best from their Windows 8 PC.

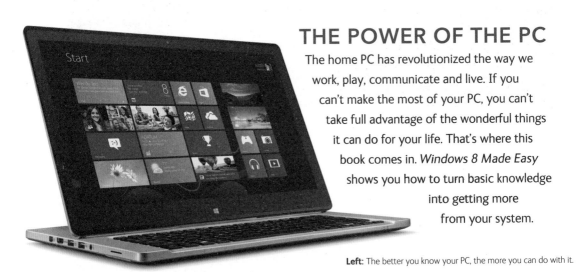

THE POWER OF THE PC

The home PC has revolutionized the way we work, play, communicate and live. If you can't make the most of your PC, you can't take full advantage of the wonderful things it can do for your life. That's where this book comes in. *Windows 8 Made Easy* shows you how to turn basic knowledge into getting more from your system.

Left: The better you know your PC, the more you can do with it.

GAME-CHANGING IDEAS

If you're not using your PC to its fullest capabilities, you're missing out on huge improvements to your hobbies and everyday activities. If you haven't heard of music streaming, then you haven't discovered the power of having 30 million songs at your fingertips that you can listen to on demand. If you haven't used cloud computing, you haven't harnessed the power of being able to access your files anywhere and haven't got the peace of mind of having your precious documents and memories safe from disaster. Windows 8.1 enables you to do these things and so much more, and this guide is your key to unlocking a new world of ideas and possibilities.

SIX IN-DEPTH CHAPTERS

Whether you're struggling to open Windows 8.1 for the first time or fed up with having only a basic knowledge of it, this guide is for you. We take you from the basics of the system to some of its best and most hidden features. You'll discover that Windows 8.1 is the perfect operating system, whether you're an absolute beginner or a seasoned IT professional.

Chapter 1 introduces all the changes in Windows 8.1, and explains why this operating system is built for a new world of devices. We show you how to take advantage of the latest advances, and which version of Windows and which type of device is best for you.

Chapter 2 takes you through the basics of the operating system, and what you can do in the first hour of turning on your PC. By the end of it, you'll be set up, secure and will be able to get on with using your PC with ultimate peace of mind. **Chapters 3** and **4** are about getting to grips with the latest apps and getting your PC connected. Windows 8.1 is nothing without the power of the Internet, so we show you how to enable this world of amazing new features.

Chapter 5 gives you the low-down on how to harness the power of your PC to enjoy games, music, photos and video – your leisure time will never be the same again!

Finally, we have a whole chapter dedicated to keeping your PC running properly, and how to overcome problems. Everyone runs into problems from time to time. This guide arms you with the knowledge of why problems arise, and walks you through the tools that not only solve them, but also prevent them from occurring in the first place.

JARGON BUSTERS

Technology is all too often packed with technical terms that can seem like another language to the uninitiated. Unfortunately, much of it is unavoidable, and understanding the terminology is an essential part of getting more from your system. That's why, in Chapter 1 (and throughout the book, as necessary), we've taken the opportunity to explain the most important terms, so you can boost your understanding of your PC.

STEP-BY-STEP GUIDES

Each section of this guide features easy-to-follow step-by-step guides, which walk you through every aspect of Windows 8.1's numerous features. *Windows 8 Made Easy* offers clear and concise explanations for every part of the operating system, with simple walkthroughs to help you every step of the way.

Hot Tips

As we guide you on your voyage of Windows 8.1 discovery, we've also provided some hot tips for getting even more out of your Windows 8.1 experience. From quick shortcuts to hacks for power users, these tips will turn you into a true Windows expert.

INTRODUCING WINDOWS 8.1

WELCOME TO WINDOWS 8.1

If you've bought a new PC, the chances are it will run Windows. Windows runs on nearly all PCs sold around the world, and is by far the most popular operating system on the planet. The first Windows operating system revolutionized PCs back in 1985, and was one of the first operating systems – with Mac OS – to have a graphical interface. This heralded the end of command-line text entry and the birth of the PCs we know today.

WHAT IS WINDOWS 8.1?

Windows 8.1 is the latest edition of the world's most popular PC operating system from Microsoft. Windows 8 was released back in October 2012 and the update to Windows 8.1 came exactly a year later.

The arrival of Windows 8 marked a huge change in the franchise to reflect the changing nature of PCs since touch-screen tablets gained popularity. There's a whole new look and interface, which means the way you use Windows 8.1 will be different to any previous version. You'll meet this new interface as soon as you open Windows – it's called the Modern User Interface – and its focus is on apps and a touch-friendly interface.

Above: The IBM PC 5150, the world's first PC, which kick-started the computing revolution, was introduced in 1981.

Above: The arrival of Windows 8 marked another chapter in PC history: the advent of the touch-screen interface.

The Role Of The Operating System

The Windows operating system is responsible for everything your PC does. Without it, programs wouldn't be able to run, nor would you be able to access the Internet or do any of the incredible things your PC can do.

Hot Tip

Don't get confused by the blank yet attractive Windows lock screen. Just tap the space bar, spin the mouse wheel or swipe upwards to reveal the login box.

Above: Your PC contains a complex mass of technology that helps connect you to the outside world, so treat it kindly!

Without an operating system, the bundle of wires, microchips and circuitry that make up your PC would be useless. All that technology is designed to run one program – the operating system – which in turn acts as the environment for all the programs running on your PC.

The New Era Of PCs

Back in the old days, PCs were made up of the tower, screen, keyboard and mouse, and even when laptops rose to prominence, the idea was still the same. However, devices such as the iPhone and iPad have changed the way we use PCs.

In a few years from now, PCs will all have touch screens as the old keyboard and mouse disappear. Windows 8.1 recognizes that trend. It makes it easy for people who use touch screens, no matter how large their fingers, so helping the Windows operating system to stay relevant on machines in the future.

Every time Windows is updated, you get a whole new set of features and Windows 8.1 is no different. The main difference is the introduction of apps, with which any user of modern tablets and smartphones will be more than familiar.

Hot Tip

Haven't moved to Windows 8 yet? Check out an upgrade version from Windows 7 rather than having to buy a new PC or an expensive box copy in stores.

WHAT'S NEW IN WINDOWS 8.1?

After the initial release of Windows 8 came an update, which fixed some issues and complaints with the original operating system. This added a whole new set of features and some minor usability tweaks. Windows 8.1 is a free update to any existing users, so there's no need to fork out extra for all those new features.

Windows 8.1 Features

- Apps from the Windows Store
- New Start screen with live updates

Hot Tip

If you're still on Windows 8, you will find your free upgrade to Windows 8.1 in the Windows Store. Just tap on the app and it will be waiting for you, front and centre. Just tap the Windows 8.1 tile in the store and it will be downloaded and installed. It's a large file, and can take an hour or more to complete.

Above: The Windows 8.1 Start screen is your gateway to a whole new Windows experience.

- Built-in web storage
- Familiar desktop area
- Works with a mouse and keyboard
- Full support and compatibility with programs
- Works with nearly all hardware
- Built for touch PCs and tablets
- Built-in web search
- Faster boot times
- Better performance on the same hardware

> **Hot Tip**
> Shut down Windows 8.1 more quickly by pressing Win + X, tap or click 'Shut down or sign out' and select the option you need.

Windows 8.1 Features

Windows 8.1 packs in a host of updates, making it a real addition to your everyday experience. Changes include:

- The Start button, which returns from exile to offer an easy way to open the Start screen.
- Boot to the desktop first
- Support for 3D printing

- Updates to all Windows apps
- Add photos to the lock screen
- Support for four apps on screen at once and resizing windows to any dimension
- Search within apps
- Fingerprint security to protect files

Above: Windows 8.1 brings back the familiar Start button in the lower-left corner of your screen.

WINDOWS 8.1 VERSIONS EXPLAINED

Windows 8.1 doesn't just come in one flavour. There are different versions for home users, businesses and a low-power version, which is used on the latest tablets. Each version has different features: here, we take you through the Windows 8.1 family.

WINDOWS 8.1 HOME

Windows 8.1 Home is the everyday edition that will serve most users perfectly adequately. You'll find this version pre-installed on most PCs found in stores and online.

What Do You Get?

Windows 8.1 Home has all the main features, from the ability to run any Windows application, access to the Windows Store and full use of the Start screen and traditional desktop. Windows 8.1 Home is compatible with keyboard and mouse as well as with touch-screen devices, and has built-in security too.

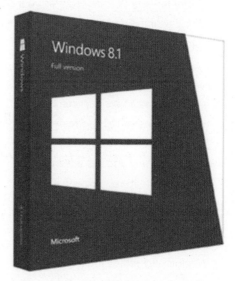

Above: Windows 8.1 Home is the most common version of the OS, and is obtainable through an upgrade.

How Do You Get It?

The most popular way for new users to get Windows 8.1 is to buy a new PC, and all systems will come with the OS pre-installed as part of the package. However, buying new gear isn't the only way to get Windows 8.1 on your system. You can also upgrade from Windows 7 by heading to http://windows.microsoft.com/en-gb/windows/buy

WINDOWS 8.1 PROFESSIONAL

The Professional edition of Windows 8.1 is aimed at business users, who need additional features compared with people using their PCs for ordinary home-computing tasks.

What Do You Get?

In Windows 8.1 Professional, you get everything that comes with the Home edition, as well as added business features. The first is BitLocker, which is an advanced encryption feature for your PC that keeps all your files behind an impenetrable wall, in case your laptop or tablet is lost or stolen.

As well as beefed-up security, Windows 8.1 Pro users can connect remotely to their PC, making files and folders accessible from anywhere in the world. Windows 8.1 Professional also has advanced networking features for connecting to corporate intranets.

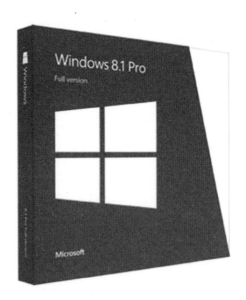

Above: The Pro version offers enhanced security as well as a host of networking features.

How Do You Get It?

Windows 8.1 Professional can be bought in stores and downloaded as an upgrade from Windows 7 and Windows 8.

WINDOWS 8.1 N AND WINDOWS 8.1 PRO N

Only available in certain European countries, these are special versions of Windows 8.1 without various Microsoft media technologies (such as Windows Media Player) so you can choose your own.

WINDOWS 8.1 ENTERPRISE

Windows 8.1 Enterprise is mainly for large organizations such as schools or businesses, typically with 20 or more people.

What Do You Get?

The Enterprise edition comes with really advanced features such as the ability to lock down the entire system or restrict parts of the operating system. Only those looking after large organizations and copious amounts of business data need worry about Enterprise.

How Do You Get It?

To get Windows 8.1 Enterprise, you need to buy a licence that covers the size of your business and every computer. It's a somewhat complex task, but you can learn more at www.microsoft.com/licensing

Above: Windows Enterprise is a feature-rich system, which can be run on all types of PC, from tablets to desktops.

WINDOWS RT

Who's It For?

Windows RT is the other version of Windows 8.1 you're likely to see on the shelves. It has more in common with mobile phone operating systems, and can only run on tablets with low-power chips.

Above: Windows RT is designed to run on thin and light PCs, such as tablets, that are used on the go.

What Do You Get?

Windows RT machines tend to operate at lower power than traditional PCs, so you get dramatically improved battery life. What's more, any Windows RT PC comes with Office 2013 RT, a touch-enabled version of Office, so you get Word, Excel and PowerPoint as standard – the only version of Windows to enjoy that luxury. However, there are some downsides. Windows RT machines cannot run traditional Windows apps, and are instead limited to the ones from the Windows Store. This means the older software you have won't work.

How Do You Get It?

You can't buy Windows RT off the shelf, but as it only works on specific hardware, few should need to. The only way to get Windows RT is to buy a low-power tablet, but check the spec sheet before you buy to make sure you know which version you're getting.

HARDWARE REQUIREMENTS FOR WINDOWS 8.1

If you're upgrading to Windows 8.1, you need to make sure your PC is up to scratch. Windows 8.1 is actually less demanding on your PC's hardware than its predecessor Windows 7, so if you have a last-generation system, you should be fine to upgrade.

Windows 8.1 upgrade path				
Which Windows 7 edition do you have?	Can Upgrade to Windows RT?	Can upgrade to Windows 8.1?	Can upgrade to Windows 8.1 Pro?	Can upgrade to Windows 8.1 Enterprise?
Enterprise	No	No	No	Yes (Volume Licence)
Ultimate	No	No	Yes	No
Professional	No	No	Yes	Yes (Volume Licence)
Home Premium	No	Yes	Yes	No
Home Basic	No	Yes	Yes	No
Starter	No	Yes	Yes	No

Check Your System

There is a handy tool on the Microsoft website that can analyze your system and check your hardware. Just go to http://bit.ly/1crsJBX and download the Windows 8.1 Upgrade Assistant.

Using the tool on the Windows website is an easy way to check your system, but if you don't have access to the Internet, or need an at-a-glance list, below you'll find everything you need.

Processor

To run properly, your PC will need a 1.0 GHz (gigahertz) (or faster) processor. However, it's recommended that your computer's processor should be a dual-core model. Most PCs from the last four years will have the required processor, but if yours is older, it would be unwise to upgrade.

RAM

You will need a minimum of 1 GB (gigabyte) of RAM to run Windows 8.1, but 2 GB or more is advisable. You can check the amount of RAM you have in Windows 7 or Window XP by clicking the Start button, right-clicking Computer and then choosing Properties.

Hard-Disk Space

Installing Windows 8.1 will take up between 16 GB and 32 GB of hard-disk space, and you can check how much you have left by right-clicking your C: drive in My Computer (in Windows XP, Windows 7 or Windows Vista) and choosing Properties. If you have less than 100 GB of free space, it's advisable to have a clear out, or avoid a new installation.

Right: Check your PC to see if it has enough RAM to run Windows 8.1.

Graphics Card

This is where things get complicated. Windows 8.1 requires a Microsoft DirectX 9 graphics device, which should be standard on any PC from the last four years. If your PC is older, make sure you take the online test.

Touch Screen

If you want to start using Windows 8.1 to its full potential, but don't own a touch screen, there are external touch screen monitors available, which can breathe new life into a desktop PC.

Above: If your PC isn't touch screen, add a touch-screen monitor to it instead.

DEVICES

Windows 8.1 has opened up a huge number of new styles of hardware, way beyond the traditional desktop PC. Read on for the types of Windows 8.1 devices on the market, and which one is right for you.

WHICH DEVICE TO CHOOSE?

PCs come in all shapes and sizes, from the traditional desktop or tower PC to the all-in-one or laptop.

Hot Tip

Desktop PCs are highly customizable, and you can also upgrade individual parts very easily in the future, which means you can make good savings.

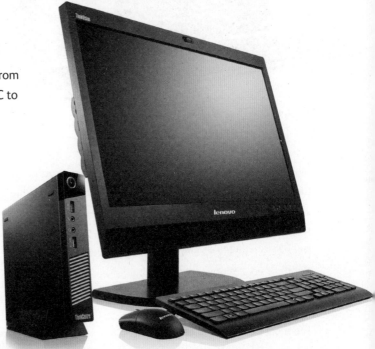

Above: A desktop costs less and offers more power and storage than a laptop or tablet.

Desktop PC

The classic desktop PC has waned in popularity due to people's desire for portability, but it's still the main choice for gamers and those using a home office. The desktop usually consists of a tower that requires a separate screen, mouse and keyboard. They don't usually have touch screen capabilities, but will offer more processing power for your money.

Above: All-in-ones are great for home use.

All-in-one PC

This type of PC has replaced the desktop in many cases. An all-in-one PC looks exactly how it sounds – all the components can be found in the same unit as the screen, so you just need to attach a keyboard and mouse. They're typically 20 in (50 cm) or larger, yet take up less desk space than a desktop unit.

All-in-one PCs have also changed recently to incorporate touch screens, and they're often aimed at home users who want a PC in areas such as the kitchen as well as the office. A touch screen all-in-one PC is also a great tool for children, as the big screen is easy to use and there are plenty of educational apps available.

Laptop

The most popular type of Windows PC, the laptop opens up to show a screen, keyboard and trackpad. They have batteries so they can be used away from the mains, which means you can use a laptop wherever you need.

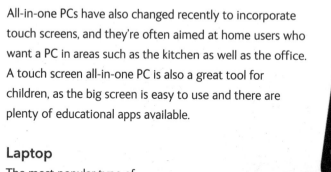

Above: Laptops offer fast performance and are good multitaskers.

Confusingly, most laptops are still too heavy to be used on a lap, with most budget systems weighing in excess of 2.5 kg, which isn't ideal for those on the move all day. Most ordinary laptops are 15.6 in (39.5 cm) in size, although there are some larger ones at 17 in (43 cm). These laptops tend to be called 'desktop-replacements', as their bulky size means they will rarely leave the house on a day-to-day basis, but can still be taken on holidays or weekends away.

Hot Tip

Don't be fooled by the portability promised by laptops. Many in the budget range are far from comfortable to carry around all day. If you want to slip your laptop into a bag and take it on the move, make sure it's under 2.5 kg.

Ultrabook

A new type of premium laptop, often known as a sleekbook, these are normally 11–14 in (28–35.5 cm) in size and feature lower-power processors that make them far lighter than normal laptops. Their low power means that Ultrabooks enjoy longer battery life, but can

Hot Tip

Many of the latest Ultrabooks come with a built-in touch screen. On the one hand, it's a great way to use Windows 8.1 at its best, but on the other, the added features drive up price and weight, and touch-screen laptops aren't as comfortable to use as tablets. Think hard about whether you will use the touch screen before forking out.

Above: Ultrabooks are light, battery-efficient and incredibly thin.

struggle with really demanding tasks like photo editing. They also tend to be much more expensive and some have touch screens.

Hybrid PC

The hybrid PC crosses the divide between laptop and tablet. These devices have the same processors as Ultrabooks and tend to have detachable keyboards and touch screens. The idea is that you use it as a tablet until you need to get down to work, when you add the keyboard for typing tasks. They tend to be small –10–12 in (25–30 cm) – but the reduced size can make the keyboard cramped to use.

Left: Hybrids offer portability and functionality.

Tablet

Without a keyboard as standard, tablets tend to run Windows RT, the version of Windows 8.1 that's designed for low-cost and small form-factor tablets. Not all tablets run Windows RT and the mobile-phone-style processor chips that come with it. Confusingly, some Windows 8.1 tablets feature full processors, and the clue is often in the name. For example, Microsoft Surface Pro uses a normal PC processor, while Surface RT costs less but is much more limited.

> **Hot Tip**
>
> Check the version of Windows 8.1 you're getting on your tablet. Check out our guide to Windows versions on pages 21–24.

Above: Some tablets, such as the one pictured, offer a full version of Windows 8.1, while others run the RT version.

Phones

There is a range of Windows phones available, which run Windows Phone 8.1 rather than Windows 8.1. Windows phones are great for people who use Windows 8.1, as they share apps and information, but it's not essential to have one. Most Windows 8.1 apps and services have Android and iOS counterparts.

Left: Windows Phone 8.1 is the third generation of the Windows Phone mobile OS.

WINDOWS TERMINOLOGY EXPLAINED

Navigating Windows can be challenging for the uninitiated, but fear not. Here's all the jargon explained to get you started.

Lock Screen

The Windows 8.1 welcome screen, which appears when the computer first boots. You will be asked to enter your password here if you're using a Microsoft account.

Start Screen

This is the new main screen in Windows 8.1, which is sometimes referred to as the Modern UI (User Interface). All your apps are here, but you need to hit the Windows key on your keyboard to return to the familiar desktop. Alternatively, there's a Desktop tile on this menu. Swipe left or right to see more apps.

Above: Pictured is the interactive Start screen, from which all your files, apps and other services are accessed.

Desktop

The desktop is the classic Windows look, with less significance in Windows 8, and is the backdrop when working in windows. Icons for your programs will appear here, and running applications can be found on the taskbar at the bottom. The background of the desktop is called your wallpaper.

Start Button

The Windows icon at the bottom-left of the desktop screen. Tap or click to return to the Start screen.

Window

This is the innovative feature that Windows took its name from in the 1980s. Everything you do is contained within a window, whether you're playing a game or looking at files on a USB stick. You can open, close, hide and switch between windows at will.

Window Snapping

In Windows 8.1, you can snap windows to either side of the screen, so apps and folders can be used side-by-side. To snap an app or desktop window, drag the title bar (or top of a Windows app) to the left or right edge of your screen. The window will then snap into place. If you're happy with the position, just release the mouse button.

Above: A pro of snap view is that two apps can be open on the same screen, allowing you to work on both at once.

Maximize/Minimize

In the top-right corner of a window, on the title bar, are two icons. Maximizing opens the window to its largest dimensions, normally filling the screen. Minimizing hides it altogether. It can be returned by tapping or clicking the taskbar.

Taskbar

The bar along the bottom of the desktop is called the taskbar. It gets its name because every 'task' (program or function that you're performing) can be found here. Hovering over an icon will open a preview of that task, and you can switch between different tasks – such as two Internet Explorer windows. At the right of the taskbar is the time.

Title Bar

At the top of a window is a long bar. This is the title bar, and you can click this to drag the window around. There will also be 'buttons' to close the window (a red 'X') and the minimize/maximize buttons.

Toolbar

Windows will often have toolbars, which have more options to explore. The toolbar will be found at the top, under the title bar, but not in the main window itself.

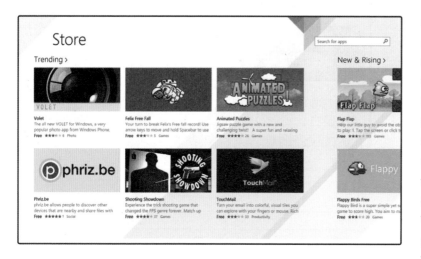

Above: Windows 8.1 comes preloaded with apps, such as Mail, Photo and Music; the Windows Store offers many more, in categories including Entertainment, Travel and Education.

Apps

Apps (applications) are small programs. The word 'app' can refer to any small utility you open, but most commonly, they're the programs that open when you click items on the Start screen. You can download more apps in the Windows Store and most of them are free.

Icons

These are small pictures that represent a link to a program or app. You will see icons on the desktop and taskbar.

Tile

The icon on the Start screen that launches apps in Windows 8.1.

Groups

Tiles on the Start screen can be arranged into a group and named. You can move entire groups of tiles around the Start screen as needed.

Windows Store

This is the place to download and buy apps in Windows. The Windows Store can be accessed from the Start screen.

Charms

Quick links to sharing, devices, settings and the search facility are known as 'charms' and are shown on the right-hand side of the screen. You can make the charms appear by moving your mouse to the bottom-right corner, or, if you're using a touch screen, sliding your finger from the right-hand edge of the screen to the middle.

Trackpad

The touch-sensitive pad found on laptops, for controlling the cursor.

Gesture

This is a shortcut for performing an action with your hand in Windows 8.1. Gestures can be made on touch screens or on some laptops' trackpads. Dragging two fingers down the trackpad to scroll a page down is an example of a gesture (for more on gestures, *see* pages 93–95).

Dragging

Dragging an item moves it about on the screen, or from one window to another. Click and hold an item to capture it, and move the mouse while holding down to drag it to its intended position.

Cursor

The pointer that you move around the screen.

File

Any document, image, song or movie will be stored as a single element called a file.

Folder

This is the area in which files are stored. Folders are used for organization, and a new one can be created at will by right-clicking on the desktop or any existing folder, and choosing New > Folder.

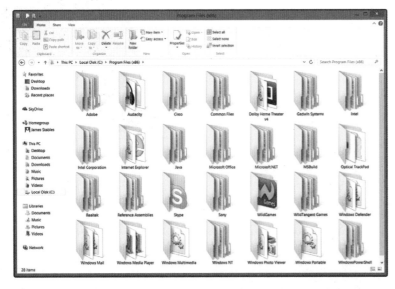

Above: Organize your data by storing it in files and folders: it's then easy to find.

Properties

To find out more about a file or folder, access the Properties menu. This can reveal all sorts of information, from the size of an item to when it was last modified.

Left-Click

The main way of selecting any item in Windows. A single left-click on your mouse will select an item, while double-clicking will open it. You can also left-click by tapping a touch screen or the main part of the trackpad. Dragging is also done via the left mouse button.

Above: The Properties menu will reveal all about a file or folder.

Right-Click

This is the standard method of accessing more options in Windows. Right-clicking will generally open a context menu, and can be done by clicking files or within folders or on the desktop. Right-clicking on touch screens is done by tapping and then holding for three seconds.

Utilities

These are programs built into the operating system that help you manage the way your PC runs. There are all sorts of utilities, from cleaning up your hard drive to removing programs and managing your hardware.

Update

A new version or addition to the Windows operating system, which is delivered via the Internet.

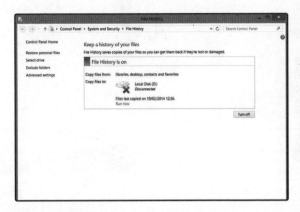

Above: File History is a useful utility, saving copies of your files.

WHAT CAN I DO WITH WINDOWS 8.1?

A Windows PC is one of the most diverse pieces of technology money can buy. From getting online for the first time to running a business with thousands of employees, Windows is used around the world by every imaginable type of user. Its open and compatible nature means you can do almost anything with a Windows PC.

SURF THE WEB

Your Windows PC is a gateway to a world of rich web content. Once connected to a home Internet network, either by plugging into your router or connecting wirelessly, you can use Internet Explorer to surf the World Wide Web. What's

Hot Tip

Use the Windows key on your desktop to toggle quickly between the Start screen and desktop, or between other apps.

Above: Windows 8.1 has many apps that make it easy to access the Internet in a variety of ways.

more, using the News, Sports, Email and other apps on the Start screen will bring the web to you, with clever feeds and tiles updating with live information as soon as you're connected.

SEND EMAIL

There's no better way to get connected than with email, and it's at the heart of Windows 8.1. You can find a Mail application on the Start screen and, because Windows is open and compatible, you can download alternatives from the Windows Store or the web.

KEEP UP WITH THE LATEST NEWS

The News app on the Start screen automatically brings headlines to your desktop, and there are plenty of other news apps to keep you informed. Bookmarking your favourite web pages will also make it easy to access the latest news, enabling you to save time and stay organized.

Above: The Photo app allows you to edit your photos, using the options shown here.

ENJOY YOUR PHOTOS

Whether you're a keen creative snapper or just enjoy a few family photos, Windows 8.1 is the perfect operating system for you. It brings all your photos together in one place and is the perfect way to enjoy flicking through your snaps. As it is designed for touch screens, it's like having your own photo album to browse, and you can quickly call up photos to the full screen.

LISTEN TO MUSIC

Windows 8.1 provides multiple ways to listen to music, making it one of the best entertainment systems out there. There's the Xbox Music app, which lets you search and listen

Hot Tip

Windows 8.1 gives you control over the size of your app tiles on the Start screen. Right-click on a tile or press and hold using a touch-screen device. Choose 'Resize' from the bottom menu, and then choose a size from the list. Major apps can be expanded to 'large' and 'wide', meaning they take up more room.

to music from the Internet, even if you haven't bought it. If you have downloaded music, Windows Media Player can find your files, organize and play them. That's not all. Thanks to the open and compatible nature of Windows 8.1's web browser, you can listen to music online, free!

WATCH TV AND MOVIES

Like the Xbox Music service, Windows 8.1 also has the Xbox Video service. It's a store jam-packed with top movies, which can be rented or bought. The Xbox Video store is more than just a shop; it will also play any files you already own.

> ## Hot Tip
> Love games? Head to the Windows Store, where you'll find hundreds of them, many of which are free to download.

PLAY GAMES

Windows 8.1 is a great platform for games and there's a variety of ways to play. If the word 'gaming' conjures images of teenagers playing death matches in their bedrooms, think again. The Windows Store is brimming with all sorts of games, from simple puzzle games such as chess and solitaire to more immersive 3D titles. What's more, if you have an Xbox, you can add your Xbox Live account to the games app and access your gamer score, avatar and friends' list.

STAY IN TOUCH WITH FRIENDS

Social networking is at the heart of Windows 8.1, with 'baked-in' Facebook and Twitter integration and dedicated apps. What's more, Windows has a People app, where contacts can be pulled in from across different services, making it even easier to stay in touch with people.

Above: The People app shows all your friends' latest updates and posts.

Above: With the Skype app, it's easy to keep in touch with friends or family who are far away.

VIDEO CHAT

For those with families and friends spread out across the country or even the world, video chatting has been one of the biggest benefits of tech. With most Windows PCs having built-in cameras and official support for Skype in Windows 8.1, it's never been easier to catch up with loved ones, 'face to face'.

CREATE DOCUMENTS

Microsoft Office has always been the staple of PC users and, while it's not included in Windows 8.1 (only Windows RT), it's still the best experience for Windows users. If you don't fancy forking out for Office, there are other free options:

Microsoft OneDrive

If you don't have a copy of Word on your PC, you can use an online version. Log into the OneDrive (formerly known as SkyDrive) and you can create documents using a web browser version of Word. The files can then be accessed via the OneDrive app on your Windows 8.1 Start screen.

OpenOffice

This is a free-to-use version of Office, which you download as an app. It looks like Office from ten years ago, but has advanced features and will adequately service most people's needs.

Google Drive

Google has a built-in word processor and spreadsheet apps, which have most of the basic functions you'll need. Being totally online, your files can be accessed anywhere and are autosaved; the downside is, if you don't have an Internet connection you won't be able to get at them.

PRINT YOUR DOCS

Windows has always been one of the best operating systems for connecting devices such as printers and scanners. Windows 8.1 makes it easy to connect a printer, be it wired or wireless.

Hot Tip

You can share a printer connected to your Windows 8.1 computer with other PCs on your network, using the HomeGroup feature.

Above: A HomeGroup network allows you to share files and devices.

CREATE EASY HOME NETWORKS

With a Windows PC you can easily connect other computers in your home to each other, letting you share files and access media such as photos and music. Most homes have more than one laptop or PC these days, so linking them together makes life so much easier.

STAY SAFE ONLINE

While Windows has a reputation of being less secure than Mac or Linux systems, it's actually packed with built-in features to keep you safe. User Account Control prevents any installation without your explicit permission, and Windows Defender, a built-in utility that's been revamped in Windows 8.1 to become a fully fledged security suite, offers you out-of-the-box protection.

Hot Tip

While Windows Defender offers decent protection when starting out, there are better free security suites available online. Try AVG Antivirus (free.avg.com) or Avast (www.avast.com) for improved security for your PC.

Hot Tip

Windows can back up your files every ten minutes, which means you'll never lose a devastating amount of data. You can change the frequency in the File History menu.

PROTECT YOUR FILES

Windows 8.1 can keep all your files safe and sound with easy automatic backups. You can choose exactly which files you'd like to have backed up, and create a custom schedule to make sure they're safely stowed in case the unthinkable happens. What's more, you can schedule your backups to run overnight, so they don't affect your work.

INTRODUCING THE START SCREEN

Windows 8.1's new look may be daunting for those used to the plain desktop in Windows 7 and Windows XP, but if used the right way, it can open up a whole new computing experience. Let us guide you around the new-look Windows.

THE WINDOWS 8.1 START SCREEN

1 Charm Bar

The Charm bar and all its useful secrets are hidden from plain view. You can reveal it by swiping in from the right on a touch-screen device, moving your mouse to the bottom right-hand corner of the screen or hitting Win + C on the keyboard.

2 Search

The first element on the Charm bar is Search. This charm brings up a box in which you can type what you're looking for. If you're in the Start menu or any part of the new-look Windows 8.1 interface, you can save time by just typing what you need, without navigating to the Search charm at all!

③ Share

When using any app or service in Windows, using the Share charm will give you options for sending content to others. What you can share is dependent on the app you're using, but all sharing options can easily be found in one place.

④ Start

If you need to get back to the Start screen at any time, you can hit this charm to be returned in double-quick fashion. It is particularly useful for those using touch-screen devices that don't have a Windows key on the keyboard.

⑤ Devices

If you have connected devices, this charm enables you to interact with them in one handy place. From USB sticks to printers and second screens, the Devices charm makes it easy to print from within apps or to play content such as videos to other devices on your network.

⑥ Settings

The Settings charm does most of the work the old control panel did, but in a much more comprehensive way. You get quick links to customizations or you can hit PC Settings in the bottom right corner to bring up a settings menu.

Hot Tip

Windows 8.1 will search your PC, your OneDrive and the web when you type a query into the Search charm, but you can modify this. Go to Change PC settings, Search and apps and Search to customize what it displays.

Hot Tip

If you miss the melée of the old Control Panel, it still has pride of place on the Start screen. Just summon the Charm bar and hit Settings, but check the list of quick links in the right-hand panel. Tapping or clicking the Control Panel option will bring back this trusty old friend.

7 Time and date

When the Charm bar is in view, you also get a system box. The time and date dominates this black panel, which can be accessed with a swipe from the right or placing the mouse in the bottom right-hand corner.

8 Battery level

This box also contains some other useful information, again accessed when summoning the Charm bar. If you're using a laptop or tablet device, you can see the status of the battery level, or the progress of your charging.

Hot Tip

Pinch in on the screen if you're using a touch screen or use the Windows key + the minus key to reduce the size of Start-screen tiles, so you can see more on screen.

Option bar — 10
Desktop — 13
Apps — 12
User — 11

Charm bar — 1
Search — 2
Share — 3
Start — 4
Devices — 5
Settings — 6

Wireless — 9
Battery level — 8

Time and date — 7
Live tiles — 14
Background theme — 15

9 Wireless

If you're connected to a wireless network, you'll get an icon with some bars, a bit like the signal on a mobile phone. Like a phone, the number of bars will signify the strength of your connection, so if only one bar is showing, you may have speed problems or dropouts.

10 Options bar

By swiping up from the bottom, or pressing the Start menu, you can bring up the Options bar. What you will see will be tailored to the app you're using. On the Start screen, you can get a list of all available apps, and options to unpin app tiles or uninstall them altogether.

Hot Tip

Swipe down, or click the down arrow on the Start screen, to get a full list of the installed apps in Windows 8.1. You can then choose what to have on your main screen, keeping it tidy and organized just how you want.

Above: When you install a new app from the Windows Store, it'll appear in the Apps view.

⑪ User

Your username and display picture will be shown in the top-right of the Start screen. This isn't just a pretty picture, however, and you can click this to change your personal settings, lock your PC or log out altogether.

⑫ Apps

Apps will be displayed on the Start screen, and you can drag the tiles around to have it set up however you need it.

⑬ Desktop

To get to the traditional Windows desktop, there's a tile on the Start screen. Its design will mirror that of your desktop wallpaper.

⑭ Live tiles

Some tiles are just icons for the app but others have special powers. The Mail app will cycle through the sender and subject lines, for example, and the Photos app will show off your snaps.

⑮ Background theme

The colourful background of the Start screen looks fantastic, but you don't have to be stuck with one colour. You can change it all using the Settings charm, and Windows 8.1 offers loads more functionality.

Hot Tip

You can dual-boot Windows 7 and Windows 8, and run them side by side. Just create a new partition on your PC using the Computer Management tool, then install the other operating system on the newly created disk. When you start your PC, you'll get a choice of which one you want to use.

INTRODUCING THE DESKTOP

The addition of the Start screen might dominate the Windows 8.1 experience, but the old desktop is only one click or tap away. While the apps of Windows 8.1 might offer more fun, the desktop is still an essential part of getting things done, so with that in mind, let's look around.

THE WINDOWS 8.1 DESKTOP

1 Desktop

The desktop is the big wide open space for all your windows, files and folders to be opened on.

2 Background

The desktop has a customizable background, which, unlike the Start screen, you're free to change to anything you want. You can have one of the stunning images included with Windows 8.1, a picture of your family or anything you like from the Internet.

3 Icons

Your desktop can have any file, folder or shortcut to a program, so everything's laid out as you need it.

Hot Tip

If you see a picture you like on the Internet, just right-click it and choose Set as background. However, it will have to be the same size as your screen to display correctly. It's best to look on websites dedicated to desktop wallpapers to get the right size.

4 Taskbar

The bar running along the bottom is the taskbar. All running programs can be opened and closed from here.

5 Pinned programs

You can pin programs to the taskbar so they can be launched quickly. Just drag any program's icon to the bar to keep it there and right-click to remove it.

Hot Tip

Right-click the taskbar and uncheck Unlock taskbar if the option is turned on. You can then click and drag the taskbar to whichever edge of the screen you want.

Icons
3

Desktop
1

Background
2

13
Internet
Explorer

12
Recycle
bin

10
Start
button

11
File
explorer

5
Pinned
programs

4
Taskbar

7
On-Screen
keyboard

8
Time and date

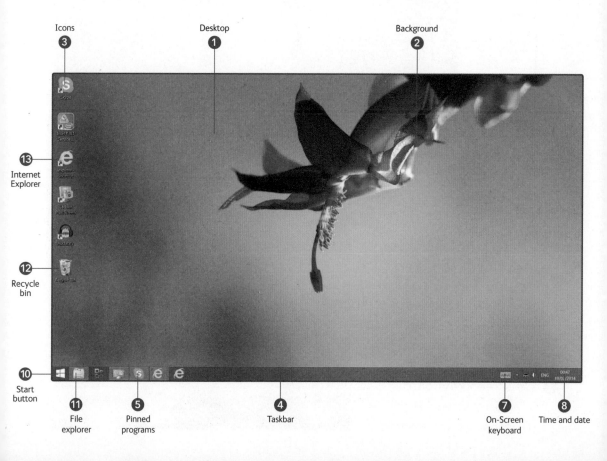

Above: Jump List menus get you to previously visited locations, files or documents, letting you work more quickly.

6 Lists

When an item in Windows 8.1 is pinned to the taskbar, it can benefit from Jump Lists. Just right-click any item to access the list, which can include shortcuts to regular features and associated files and documents.

7 On-screen keyboard

In Windows 8.1, you can summon a keyboard at anytime

Above: The on-screen keyboard is useful for those who don't have access to a physical version, such as tablet users.

by pressing the icon on the taskbar. You can then toggle different types of keyboard, so you can use whatever is comfortable.

8 Time and date

You'll find the time and date displayed on the right-hand side of the taskbar at all times. You can click it to make adjustments and get an at-a-glance calendar.

9 Running tasks

You can see all background apps and tasks that are running in the notification area, on the right of the taskbar. This can be Bluetooth connectivity, security suites or the software running your sound card, among other things. You can change what you see here by clicking Customize.

⑩ Start button

The Start button was returned in the Windows 8.1 update, and it's now another way to get back to the Start screen.

Above: File Explorer (previously Windows Explorer) allows you to view your files and folders, all in one window.

⑪ File Explorer

This icon will open a new window, which will enable you to access the traditional folders, such as Documents, Downloads and Pictures, where you can browse and organize your files.

⑫ Recycle bin

To delete items, just drag them to the bin. Here they will remain until you right-click and empty the folder, after which they will be gone for ever.

⑬ Internet Explorer

Windows 8.1's default browser, Internet Explorer is your gateway to the Internet. If you choose an alternative browser, it will be displayed here.

⑭ Return To Desktop

There's an invisible hotspot at the bottom-right, which will minimize all windows to reveal the desktop.

⑮ Charm Bar

From the traditional desktop, you can still access the Windows 8.1 Charm bar. However, when you're not using the new-look Windows 8.1 apps, the number of options at your disposal is diminished.

WINDOWS 8.1 MADE EASIER

One thing is guaranteed in Windows 8.1, and that's every option and feature has a hidden shortcut for getting it done more quickly and easily. The operating system is full of hidden time savers and, when you take the time to learn them, they really get under your skin. We show you how to make Windows 8.1 even easier to use.

ACCESS FILES AND WEBSITES WITH JUMP LISTS

Using the Windows 8.1 desktop is a great way to get more done, and the Jump List feature epitomizes how powerful this area of Windows can be. Jump Lists are a simple method of making sure everything you need is at your fingertips, and best of all, most of their power is automatic in Windows 8.1.

Accessing Jump Lists

1. First, get set up by adding your favourite Windows 8.1 programs to your desktop taskbar. Just drag icons from the desktop, or right-click (or long-press) items from the Windows Start screen and choose Pin to Taskbar.

2. To access the Jump Lists, just right-click a taskbar item. Touch screen users can long-press on the icon.

3. Each Jump List is different and tailored to the program, but each is split into three items: Frequent, Tasks and general items.

Right: Master Jump Lists, and everything you need will be just a click away.

Above: Jump Lists' Customization pane.

4. Under Frequent will be the items you use the most. In Internet Explorer, these will be the sites you visit most, while the Microsoft Word Jump List will have the most used documents. You can open the website, file or other item by clicking it, saving you time.

5. If you want to keep that item in the list permanently, then hover your cursor over the item and click the pin that appears on the right.

Customize Your Jump Lists

You can affect the way Jump Lists work to make them more useful to your needs. There's a host of quick customizations you can make, straight from the desktop.

1. You can change the number of items your Jump Lists can hold. Right-click on the taskbar (not on an icon) and click Properties.

2. Choose Jump Lists from the tabs at the top.

3. Change the number of items you want in your Jump Lists. The default is ten, but you can choose up to 99.

4. Click OK to confirm.

Do More With Jump Lists

If you want more customization of Jump Lists, you can use a third-party app. Download Jump List Launcher from the internet, which enables you to create customized lists that mix together any type of file or program on your PC.

USE THE ON-SCREEN KEYBOARD

One of the huge improvements in Windows 8.1 is its focus on touch screens, which has opened up a host of new form-factors for Windows devices. If you've invested in a Windows tablet, whether it's running Windows 8.1 or the mobile version Windows RT, the on-screen keyboard will be a huge part of your experience.

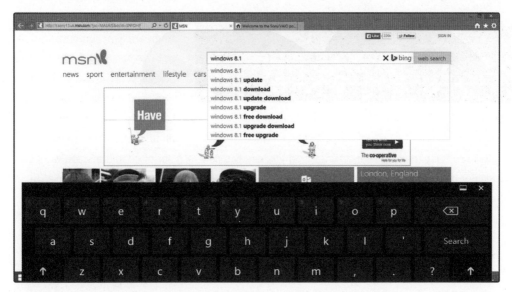

Above: Windows' on-screen keyboard is intuitive, and gives easy access to numbers and common symbols.

What Is The On-screen Keyboard?

Often, tablet devices don't have a keyboard and, in the case of many of the new Windows laptops, the tablet is detachable so it's easier to use on the move. When your keyboard isn't connected, the Windows on-screen keyboard can be used to input text instead.

Bring Up The Keyboard

The on-screen keyboard will appear when Windows thinks you want to input text and detects that you haven't got a physical one attached. However, you can summon the keyboard

Above: The split, or thumb, keyboard is perfect to use when standing up.

whenever you need it, using the icon on the taskbar. Tap it to have the keyboard appear at the bottom half of the screen.

Keyboard Language

There's not just one on-screen keyboard: you can customize it to however you want it on your device. When the keyboard is displayed on the screen, tap the icon in the bottom right-hand corner. The first option you'll see is for the language settings, and you can toggle which set of characters you want to use. For most people, this will be UK or US, but you can set up any language in the PC Settings menu, in case you need to access accents and characters not on the default keyboard.

Split View

Under these options are three options for different views. The first is the default, while the second shows the keys set to either side. This is the split keyboard, and is perfect for larger devices, where it's hard to hold and have your fingers reach to the middle of the screen at the same time.

Handwriting

The third option is for natural handwriting, which is best for users whose tablet or PC comes with a stylus input. This enables you to write emails, web addresses or any kind of text by hand, and have Windows 8.1 decipher your scrawls into editable fonts.

Hot Tip

Just like older versions of Windows, you can press Alt + F4 to shut down apps quickly and easily. It's not as useful for touch screen users, but for those who still have a mouse and keyboard, it's a massive time-saver.

MAKE YOUR PC EASIER TO USE

If you find using a PC difficult, Windows 8.1 is there to help. It's packed with customizations and tools to make your life easier. Here are just a few that will make your PC an even greater joy to use.

Make Your Screen Easier To See

If you find it hard to see particular areas of your screen, then follow these steps.

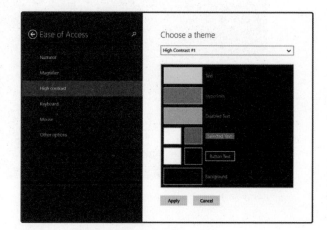

1. Find the Ease of Access Center by heading to the Search charm, choosing PC Settings and then Ease of Access.

2. Choose Magnifier from the list. This tool enlarges parts of your screen so that you can see the words and images more clearly.

Above: You can also get to accessibility settings from the desktop: press the Windows logo key + U.

3. Back in the left-hand pane, choose High contrast. If you find it hard to read text on your screen because you need more colour contrast, you can change the mode here.

4. In the Other options menu, you can turn off animations, adjust cursor thickness and make other selections to make using Windows easier on the eye.

Make Text Larger

Some people find it hard to read text on the screen, which can be a problem on devices with smaller screens such as tablets and hybrids, so here's how to make it larger:

1. Swipe in from the right edge of the screen, then choose Settings.

Above: High Contrast mode can make Windows easier for people who find computer screens hard to read.

2.   Tap or click PC and devices and then tap or click Display.

3.   Look for the More options heading. Under Change the size of apps, make sure it's set to the largest option.

Make Using The Mouse Easier

For some people, especially older users, using a mouse isn't easy. The pointer can be too small, or the white cursor can be hard to make out against the background.

1.   Return to the Ease of Access menu and choose Mouse from the list of options.

2.   From here, you can change the colour and size of mouse pointers to make things easier. The cursor will change on screen as soon as you select an option, so you can try it on for size.

3. Once you're done, just return to the
    home screen.

If using a mouse is just too awkward or difficult,
don't give up on using your PC altogether. You
can turn on mouse keys in the Ease of Access
menu, which enables the arrow keys on your
keyboard to move the pointer instead.

Make Using The Keyboard Easier

Follow these steps to customize your keyboard:

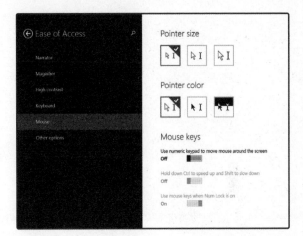

Above: The Ease of Access/Mouse menu lists many options, as
shown here, so it's simple to find one that works for you.

1. Return to the Ease of Access menu
    and choose Keyboard.

2. If you struggle with complex keyboard shortcuts such as Ctrl + Alt + Delete, you can
    turn on Sticky Keys. This means you can press key combos concurrently, but not
    simultaneously, to launch commands.

3. Toggle Keys alert you if you want to
    be alerted to pressing the Caps Lock,
    Num Lock or Scroll Lock keys. These
    notifications prevent what can be an
    annoying mistake of pressing these
    keys inadvertently.

4. When you turn on Filter Keys, Windows
    ignores it when you press the same key
    rapidly or when you press keys for several
    seconds unintentionally.

Above: The Ease of Access/Keyboard settings are invaluable for
users who struggle to press more than one key at a time.

GETTING STARTED

SETTING UP WINDOWS 8.1

It's quick to get started with Windows 8.1, but things aren't as simple as the old days when you turned on your PC and it was ready to go. Windows 8.1 uses a web-based log in, which helps unlock the new features. We show you how to install the new OS and get started.

INSTALL WINDOWS 8.1

Most people's first experience with Windows 8.1 will be via a new PC, but that's not the only way to get the new operating system. You can buy the OS on disk and install it like any other program on your PC. If you're installing Windows 8.1 from a disk or other media, follow these steps for quick and easy installation.

1. Turn on your PC so that Windows starts normally, insert the DVD or USB flash drive, then shut down your PC. Restart your PC, then press any key to boot from the DVD or USB flash drive.

2. If you restart your PC and your current version of Windows starts, you might have to open a boot menu or change the boot order in your PC's BIOS so that

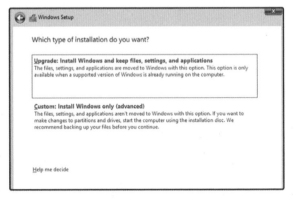

Above: Before upgrading to Windows 8.1, make sure you have backed up your files before you start the process.

your PC boots from the correct place (BIOS, or Basic Input/Output System, is a simple program which connects all your hardware and executes the launch of Windows). Turn to page 82 to see our full guide on how to change the boot priority on your Windows PC.

3. On the Install Windows page, enter your language and other preferences, then tap or click Next, then tap or click Install Windows. On the Enter the product key to activate Windows page, enter your product key.

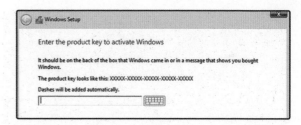

Above: It's a good idea to keep a record of your product key, in case you should ever need to reinstall the software.

4. You'll then be asked to click the partition that you want. Most systems will have a C: drive, which is for the operating system installation. If you're dual-booting, however, choose an empty partition rather than the C: drive.

Personalize Windows

First, Windows 8.1 will ask you to choose the colour for your experience and set-up. There's an array to choose from. You'll then be asked to name your PC. This is to identify it when networking. Connect your Wi-Fi by choosing it from the list. Windows will look to get settings from the web, so it's important to connect if possible.

Express Setup

You'll now see the Settings menu. You can use custom settings or express. Most users will be fine with the standard express settings, but if you want control over updates, location details and settings at this early stage, click Customize.

Hot Tip
To create a new partition on your PC, you need to use the Disk Management tool in Windows 8, which is also known as Computer Management in Windows 7 and Vista. Right-click a disk with spare capacity and choose Shrink Volume, and choose the amount of space you want to reclaim. Right-click the now-unused space and choose New Simple Volume to turn that into a separate drive.

Above: Choosing a set-up colour is one way to personalize Windows; there are more in the Personalization Gallery.

Above: Read through the settings menu before accepting it.

Hot Tip

You don't have to sign in with a Microsoft account. If you'd rather not go through the signup, you can choose to be a local user. However, this will limit a lot of the features you can access, and many apps won't work without a registered email address.

Above: Your email address will link your PC with your online life.

Once you've accepted the settings, you'll be asked to sign in with a Microsoft account. If you don't have an Internet connection, you can skip this by clicking the Local account option, from where you will be delivered to the Windows 8.1 Start screen. We recommend using a Microsoft account, so check out the next section to find out what it is and how to use it.

YOUR MICROSOFT ACCOUNT

Windows 8.1 is designed to be paired with an email address, to link your PC with your online life. By doing this, it makes your PC more secure, as well as allowing email, calendars and contacts to be delivered to your operating system to make your experience richer. Read on to find out how to set up your Windows ID.

What Is A Microsoft Account?

Any email account which is used to log in to Windows 8.1 becomes a Microsoft account, enabling a host of extra features. The email account you use doesn't have to be one of Microsoft's own services, such as Hotmail, Outlook or Live, it can be any address, such as Yahoo!, Gmail or your own personal domain.

Which Services Does It Enable?

While Windows 8.1 still works with your PC's hard drive, the web-based login means 'cloud' services are enabled. The chief cloud component is the 7 GB of storage through the OneDrive app, which enables you to keep files and photos online. Among other services which benefit from the Microsoft account is email, which is integrated into the Start screen, as well as the contacts that populate the People app and calendar entries.

Setting Up A Microsoft Account

1. Type your email address into the box provided. If you haven't got one already, or if you don't have access to the account, click Sign up for a new email address in the list at the bottom.

2. If you choose to create a new email address, you'll be asked for a small amount of personal information and to choose what email address you want.

3. You can choose the prefix – the name before the @ symbol – select from outlook.com, hotmail.com or live.com, and choose a password before clicking or tapping Next.

> # Hot Tip
>
> **When you use an existing email address for your Microsoft account, Windows 8.1 will require you to confirm the address is real by sending you an email to that account. These can often end up in your spam or junk folder, so check there if it doesn't come through.**

Above: You can use any existing email address for your Microsoft account, Outlook.com, Gmail, or Yahoo, for example.

4. Windows will then start creating your account, which can take a few minutes. You'll now be directed to the Windows Start screen. When you log into your PC in future, you'll need to use the password for your account, so don't forget it.

Above: You can link other accounts to your Microsoft account, such a Facebook one.

Above: Your email address and password are the key to unlocking info on your PC.

CHOOSE YOUR BROWSER

Your Internet browser is the program that enables you to browse the web, and lets you enter the web address and displays the website you navigate to. When you first start Windows, you'll be asked to select a browser.

How To Use The Browser Choice Feature

Browser Choice should start automatically when you start using Windows 8.1. Alternatively, tap or click the Browser Choice tile on the Start screen. In the Welcome screen, tap or click OK or Continue. In the Select your web browser screen, tap or click Install. Tap or click Tell me more for information about any of the browsers. Follow any on-screen instructions.

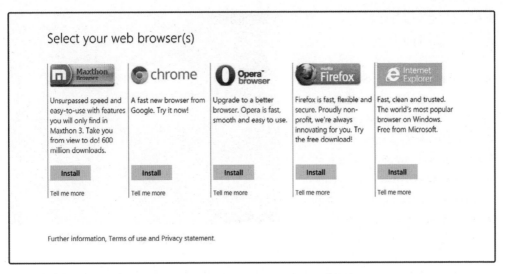

Above: Although you will be presented with a choice, Internet Explorer is Windows 8.1's default browser.

WHICH BROWSER SHOULD YOU CHOOSE?

Internet Explorer

The top choice for new users or those who use Microsoft services, Internet Explorer has the best integration with Windows 8.1, with improved use of the Jump Lists on the desktop.

Google Chrome

Best for those who use Google services such as Gmail or Google Docs, Chrome is extremely stable and is fast becoming the world's most popular browser.

Firefox

The top choice for those who like to tinker with their PCs, Firebox's huge library of add-ons and additions serve nearly any need. From RSS feeds to download managers, you can find all sorts within the huge range of plug-ins.

SET UP USER ACCOUNTS

What Are User Accounts?

A PC is rarely used by just one person, so it's handy for everyone who uses Windows to have a personal login. That's why Windows 8.1 enables every user to have their own account, which keeps files, programs and apps separate, enabling you to keep things just the way you want them.

Above: Adding another user allows that person to customize Windows 8.1 as they wish.

Set Up A New User

To get started adding family members to your Windows 8.1 PC, head to the Start screen and access the Setting charm by swiping from the right, or placing your mouse in the bottom right-hand corner. Choose PC Settings from the list and then, in the following menu, choose Users. Click or tap Add a user at the bottom of the screen.

Left: Children's accounts have built-in safety features.

Hot Tip

Windows 8.1 enables you to make special accounts for children. When creating a new account, choose Add a child's account from the list. You can also opt to set up without an email address.

STAY IN CONTROL WITH ADMINISTRATOR ACCOUNTS

If you're looking to set up accounts for your family, but are worried about letting kids or other users have access to the advanced workings of your PC, you're in luck. By default, the main Windows 8.1 account is an administrator, which means anyone using it can make changes. Any other account is a standard account, so those users won't be able to make critical amendments to the system.

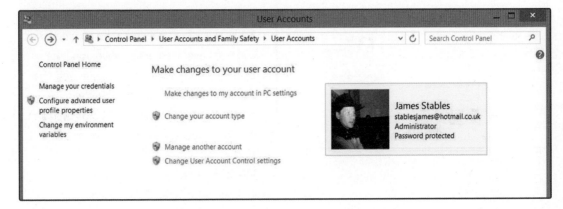

Above: Only the main account holder, or administrator, is able to make changes, such as installing new software.

Manage Your Users

Other accounts don't have to be standard, however. You can change the status of any account, upgrading and downgrading it as you please. To make changes to accounts on your Windows 8.1 PC, choose Manage another account.

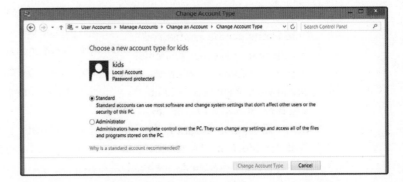

Above: As administrator, you can change the status of individual accounts at any time.

SET UP PARENTAL CONTROLS

Windows PCs are a great way for children to learn – and have fun – but using the Internet and Windows 8.1 apps can lead to inquisitive minds stumbling across things they shouldn't. That's where parental controls come in. In Windows 8.1, these features are called Family Safety. You can access it by typing 'Family Safety' while the Start screen is open and choosing it from the Settings menu. Choose an account in the list and then tick On to apply Family Safety.

Above: If each child in your family has their own account, you can tailor the Family Safety measures according to their ages.

Activity Reporting

Prevention is better than cure, but Windows 8.1 enables you to keep an eye on what your children have been doing while using the computer. Activity reporting sends you, the administrator, a report showing the most popular websites, when the PC was used and whether any apps and games were accessed.

Web Filtering

The biggest dangers for children using computers are unsuitable websites, but while active supervision is best, you can add an extra layer of protection by blocking websites. Firstly, you can choose to block all websites you deem unsuitable by clicking Web Restrictions. Alternatively, you can block specific websites.

Time Limits

If you want to limit the amount of time children can use the computer, Windows 8.1 can help with that too.

Hot Tip

Time Limits can be configured in a variety of ways. For example, you could allow children to log in with their accounts at any time of day on a Sunday, but to a maximum of an hour. Just use the Time Allowance feature in the Time Limits menu.

The Time Limits option in Family Safety lets you specify times of the day their accounts can be used, and if they're still using the computer when their time expires, they will be logged out.

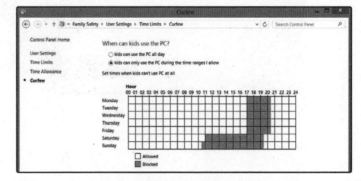

Above: Set a limit on the amount of time your child spends on the PC.

Game And App Restrictions

Playing games in Windows 8.1 can be educational and fun, but not if children get access to unsuitable content. In Family Safety, you can restrict games and apps from the Windows Store in two ways. Firstly, you can set a maximum age certification. Secondly, you can opt to restrict all apps, unless they are first vetted and allowed by you.

WINDOWS 8.1 SETTINGS

Windows 8.1 is one of the most customizable operating systems out there, and there's a host of settings at your fingertips. Tweaking settings used to involve delving into the Control Panel, which was not for the faint hearted, but the new PC Settings menu makes the most regular tweaks quick and easy.

MAKE WINDOWS 8.1 WORK YOUR WAY

To access the PC Settings menu, you need to open the Charms bar and choose Settings. A panel will appear on the right, in which you choose PC Settings. A new screen will appear with a host of options, which we'll talk you through now.

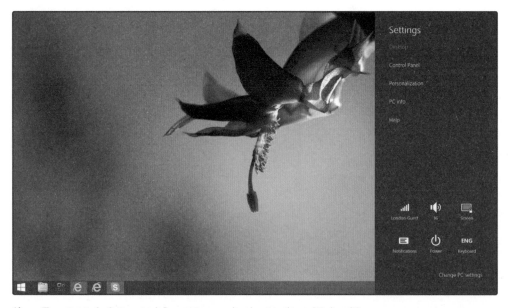

Above: The options in the Settings panel allow you to personalize almost anything in Windows 8.1.

Above: The PC and devices menu enables you to add a photo to your screen, amongst other things.

PC And Devices

A huge catch-all menu with a host of important options for every aspect of your PC. Here, you can tweak the lock screen and monitor settings, Bluetooth, the mouse and trackpad, among other options.

Accounts

This set of options enables you to manage your account and change your profile picture, as well as quickly add new users. You can also opt to use a Microsoft account to log into your PC to enrich your Windows 8.1 experience.

Search And Apps

Here, you can tweak the results from the Search charm within Windows 8.1, as well as the way in which other Charms work. There are also settings for sharing, which will let you manage the types of apps Windows 8.1 will let you share information with. What's more, you can get an idea of which apps are taking up the most room on your hard drive.

Hot Tip

When you first press the Settings button, there are a handful of quick links you can click, instead of trawling through the main PC Settings menu. One of these enables you to access the traditional Windows Control Panel, which has a far more comprehensive range of options.

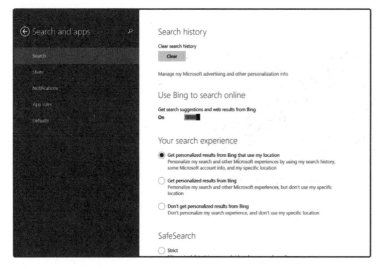

Above: The Search and apps menu allows you to personalize your search experience.

If Windows 8.1's apps are bothering you with too many alert sounds, you can turn them down in the Notifications menu. Every app is listed with a simple slider, so you can choose whether alerts are on or off. You can also turn off sounds and screen prompts here.

Privacy

This menu puts you in control of your information and data. If you're concerned about your webcam or microphone being accessed by apps, location information being broadcast, or the use of your data by apps, you can block access here.

Network

Windows 8.1 has a great way of sharing files with other PCs in your network and a host of ways to connect. The chief option is called HomeGroup and is accessible through the Network option in the PC Settings menu. You can control what's shared here, choosing between

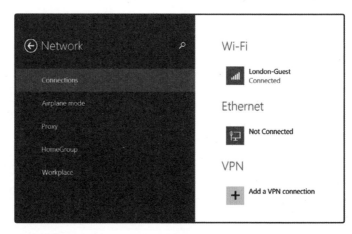

Above: Choose which network to connect to in the Network/Connections menu.

documents, music, pictures, videos and even printers. Turn to our guide on page 162.

Time And Language

You can change every aspect of Windows 8.1's time settings in this menu. You can also change the world time-zone settings here, which is very useful if you're using your PC abroad.

Ease Of Access

If you find your PC hard to use because of visual impairments, Windows 8.1 can help. You can put your Start screen into high-contrast mode, which can make options easier to see. Turn to our section on making your PC easier to use on page 59.

Update And Recovery

The final option in the list is Windows Update, which will notify you of any updates you have not yet installed, and prompt you to restart to enjoy the full benefits of the latest software improvements. If you're having PC problems, you can also reset your PC, which we outline on page 226.

Hot Tip

If you're hankering after more complex settings, press Win + X to launch a menu with quick links to Network Connections, Computer Management and more.

CUSTOMIZE WINDOWS 8.1

You can quickly make changes to the Start screen via the Settings charm, but that's not the only part of Windows you can personalize with your own stamp. The desktop is also totally customizable, with a host of options to make Windows 8.1 feel like home. To get started, just right-click on the desktop and choose Personalize.

GIVE WINDOWS 8.1 YOUR OWN STAMP

There are multiple ways that Windows 8.1 lets you customize the interface. While the Start screen is relatively plain in its design, the desktop is a place where you can really go to town.

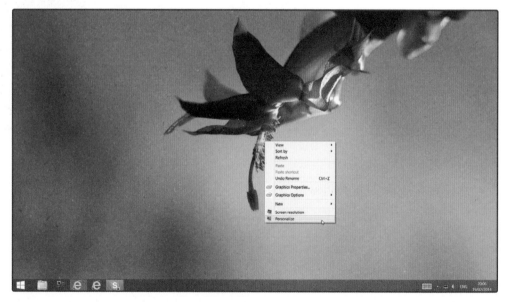

Above: The desktop is as good a place as any to start when it comes to personalizing your PC.

Windows Themes

Windows 8.1 has a variety of themes, which take over all aspects of the desktop's look. All the aspects of the theme, from the sets of multiple background images to the title bar colours, are designed to complement each other. Just click a theme to apply it and then click Save. You're not limited to the themes in the menu either. Click the link labelled Get more themes online and you can download new ones from the web.

Change Backgrounds

While the themes may look great, they don't have the personal touch of your own snaps. However, the good news is you can make any picture your desktop background.

Click Desktop background at the bottom and you'll get a view of your Pictures library. You can choose any image here, or click to browse and to navigate to a specific file's location. Alternatively, right-click any image file, even on web pages, and choose Set as desktop background.

Save Your Custom Theme

By changing Windows' colours and desktop backgrounds, you're actually creating your own

Above: You can create a custom theme which uses your own photos and allows you to you decide a matching or contrasting colour scheme.

Hot Tip

Want your desktop and Start screen to share the same background? Choose the Personalize option from the Settings charm on the Start screen and you'll see your current desktop wallpaper appear alongside the other options.

theme. When you've got everything the way you want it, you'll notice a box that says Unsaved theme in the main Personalization window. Click Save theme, give it a name, and it will be saved amongst the default Windows options.

Change Windows Colour

All windows in Windows 8.1 have a title bar, and you can customize the colour of this. You can choose any shade just by clicking Color at the bottom of the Personalize screen. Just choose any of the colours provided and then use the slider to change intensity.

Above: Alert sound annoying you? Head to the Sounds option and change away!

Change Sounds

It's not just the look of Windows that you can change. Nearly every action in Windows has a sound attached to it, and you can change those tones in the Sounds option. You can change any sound, and even replace it with your own, should you wish.

Set A Screensaver

Screensavers were designed to prevent monitor damage by leaving a still image on screen for too long, but they're a great way to add a dash of personality to your PC. Anyone familiar with the screensavers from older versions of Windows will be right at home – they have barely changed since Windows 98. Choose the screensaver from the list, and change options such as text or colour using the Settings box, and when you're done, click Apply.

Above: The Change Desktop Icons pane.

Alter Desktop Icons

The final way to customize Windows is to change the look of your desktop icons. The problem is that after a while, those icons can get bland, so why not change them by tapping into Windows 8.1's library of unused icons? In Personalization, just choose Change Desktop Icons, choose an item from the desktop, click Change Icon and then find one that suits.

Hot Tip
Played around with your icons too much? If you're sick of your new-look icons, just go back to the Change Desktop Icons menu and click the Restore Default button.

SET UP THE ESSENTIALS

Once you've got to grips with the basics of Windows 8.1, you'll want to get on with using it for everyday tasks. Whether it's setting up your printers or overcoming bugbears with the system, we show you how to get the essentials sorted, so you can get on with enjoying your PC.

BOOT STRAIGHT TO THE WINDOWS 8.1 DESKTOP

1. Go to the desktop, right-click (or press and hold) on the taskbar and choose Properties.

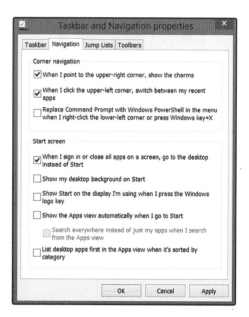

Hot Tip

If you do choose to boot straight to the desktop, you can still access Windows 8.1's new interface whenever you need. Just hit the Windows key or use the re-instated Start button to get back to the Modern UI.

2. Click or press the Navigation tab.

3. Check the box next to When I sign in or close all apps on a screen, go to the desktop instead of Start. Touch or click the OK button to confirm your choice.

When you boot up and sign into Windows 8.1, you will now be taken to the desktop instead of the Start screen. To get back to the Start screen, just click the Start button on the desktop, or use the Windows key.

Left: Boot to desktop – useful for non-touch users – is new in Windows 8.1.

INSTALL A PRINTER

One of the great things about Windows 8.1 is its compatibility with most hardware and software, which makes setting up things like printers really easy. To make the printer and PC work together, you need a piece of software known as a driver. Windows already has drivers for most printers built-in.

Above: As Windows supports most of the main printers, you probably won't have to install any special software to get up and running.

Quick Start

To install your printer, just plug it in via a USB cable. Make sure it's switched on, and wait for the hardware to be detected. You should get a notification that Windows has found an attached device and a running status of its installation. Windows 8.1 has most of the main printer brands' drivers pre-installed.

Confirm The Install

Once Windows has found the drivers and installed them, you should be ready to print. Go into an app you'd like to print from, such as Microsoft Word, choose to print and you should see it listed. Alternatively, to check that it has been installed, swipe in from the right-hand edge of the screen (or position the mouse in the bottom right), choose Settings followed by Change PC settings. Under PC and devices, tap or click Devices. If your printer is installed, it should appear under the Printers options.

Above: Head to the Add devices menu to install a new printer.

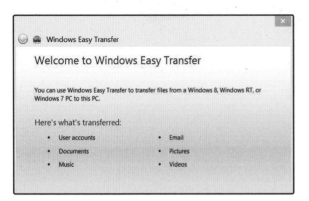

Above: Easy Transfer helps move documents in one process.

Troublesome Printers

If your printer isn't listed in Settings and you fear that it hasn't installed, there are other options. Tap or click Add a device in the Devices menu and then select your printer to install it. If it doesn't come up, check that it's switched on and you have the cable attached properly. In the event that you still can't install your printer, use the supplied software.

TRANSFER FILES FROM A WINDOWS 7 PC

Moving to a new PC is difficult enough, but transferring all your files across can be a serious hassle. Backing up everything to an external hard drive will do for documents and photos, but that doesn't help get your settings the way you like them, or things working your way.

Hot Tip

While Windows Easy Transfer can back up settings, it's inadvisable to do this in Windows 8.1. The new version of the operating system is so different to its predecessors that it can cause problems, so just stick to files.

That's where Windows Easy Transfer comes in. It backs up all your files, which can then can be uploaded into Windows 8.1 with a minimum of fuss. It is worth noting that settings for non-Microsoft software may not be included in Windows Easy Transfer, so it's best to back these up separately.

Make The Switch

First, you'll need a USB storage device with plenty of room. Plug in your drive and go to Computer in Windows and you'll be able to see how full it is. How much free space is required is completely dependent on how many files you have to back up.

Above: The external hard drive you use must have enough space for your files.

1. On your Windows 7 PC, go to the Start menu and type 'easy transfer' into the search box. When Windows Easy Transfer loads, press Next and choose USB storage from the list – provided that's the method of transfer you want to use. Windows Easy Transfer will also use CDs, DVDs and network storage.

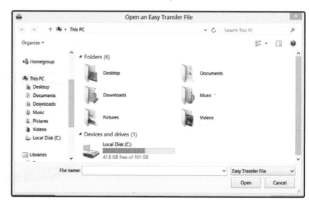

Above: Easy Transfer will estimate how much disk space is needed for your files.

2. Windows 7 will scan the PC for items you might want to back up. It puts these under the headings of User and Shared items. User files are any files, documents and images that are specific to certain users, and these will be saved under those same accounts, provided they've been created on the destination PC.

Backup Beware

Windows Easy Transfer will only work if both your systems are 32 or 64 bit. This denotes the type of system your PC is running. You can check which system your PC is running by going to the System menu, which is best accessed by searching for 'System' using the Windows 7 Search feature when clicking the Start orb, or by searching from the Windows 8.1 Start charm. If they're incompatible, then use the Backup and Restore Center in Windows 7 to save your files manually.

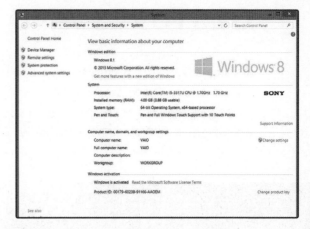

Above: The System menu will reveal if your PC has a 64-bit system.

Resurrect Your Files On Windows 8.1

If you're using Windows Easy Transfer, follow these steps to get your backup onto your new PC:

1. Go to your Windows 8.1 PC and plug in your USB device.

2. Search for 'easy transfer' on the Start screen.

3. Click Next on the first screen and you'll be presented with the question 'Have you already used Windows Easy Transfer to save your files from another PC?' Choose Yes.

4. A box will open. Go to your storage device, which will be listed in the left-hand pane, and find the Windows Easy Transfer file.

5. Press Open and you'll see a summary of the User and Shared files.

6. If your old PC had multiple user accounts and you have these set up on your new Windows 8.1 PC, click Advanced.

7. Press Transfer and have your files transferred, easily.

GESTURES AND SHORTCUTS

Windows 8.1 is full of shortcuts, and all methods of input have their own hidden tricks. These are normally the reserve of power users and may take some getting used to if you've been used to working a certain way. However, master them and you'll have Windows 8.1's power at your fingertips.

MOUSE GESTURES

Get Back To The Start Screen
Point to the bottom-left corner and click it.

Open The Charms
Point to the top-right or bottom-right corner to see charms.

See All Apps
Click the down arrow in the bottom-left corner of the Start screen.

Get To Commands And Context Menus In An Application
Right-click within the application, then click the command you want. Alternatively, right-click an item to see the options specific to that item.

Switch Between Open Apps

To switch to your most recently used application, point to the top-left corner. When the previous application appears, click the Preview window.

Above: When switching, try to direct the mouse's pointer up into the left-hand corner so it disappears.

Switch To a Different App

To switch to a different application, point to the top-left corner and then move down the edge. When the other applications appear, click the one you want.

Open The Desktop

Go to the Start screen, then click the Desktop tile.

Zoom In Or Out On Start

Move your mouse to the bottom-right corner and press the Summary View icon to get an overview of every app tile, or press Ctrl + and scroll the mouse wheel to zoom out. Click anywhere to zoom back in.

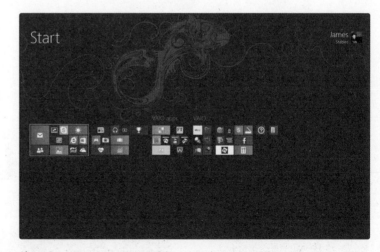

Above: By zooming out, you can see all the apps you have on your Start screen.

Hot Tip

In the taskbar Properties menu, you can turn off the hot corners, which show the charms and window-switching features. Click the Navigation tab and then untick the options at the top.

Arrange Tiles

Drag your application from the top of the screen and place it on the left or right side, then go to the Start screen and click another application.

Close Current Application

Point to the top edge of the screen, then drag the application to the bottom of the screen.

Shut Down Your PC

Point to the bottom-right corner. When the charms appear, move up, then click Settings. Click Power, then choose a shut-down option.

Close Open Apps

You can also close applications you've used recently by pointing to the top-left corner and then moving down the edge. Right-click the one you want, then click Close.

KEYBOARD SHORTCUTS

Keyboard shortcuts are combinations of key presses that are designed to save you time, and can really help you to get things done in Windows 8.1.

General Windows Shortcuts

When using Windows and its programs, there's a handful of keyboard shortcuts that will work across the board. They've been around since the earliest versions of Windows, and memorizing these will really speed up your work.

F1:	Help
Ctrl + Esc:	Open Start menu
Alt + Tab:	Switch between open programs
Alt + F4:	Quit program
Shift + Delete:	Delete item permanently
Ctrl + Alt + Delete:	Start Up Manager
Windows key + L:	Lock the computer
Ctrl + C:	Copy selected text
Ctrl + X:	Cut the selected text
Ctrl + V:	Paste selected in current location
Ctrl + Z:	Undo last action
Ctrl + B:	Make selected text bold
Ctrl + U:	Underline selected text
Ctrl + I:	Make selected text italic

Above: Alt + Tab enables you to switch between programs.

Above: Ctrl + Alt + Delete brings up the Task Manager, which shows you the programs currently running on your computer.

Windows 8.1 Keyboard Shortcuts

Because Windows 8.1 has introduced so many new features and applications, there are a host of new shortcuts. Because of the reliance on gestures and hotspots, it's actually a huge timesaver for non-touch screen users to use these commands, and it will make using Windows 8.1 a breeze.

Windows logo key + start typing:	Search your PC
Ctrl + (+) or Ctrl + (-):	Zoom in or out of Start screen
Windows key + C:	Open the charms
Windows key + F:	Open the Search charm to search files
Windows key + H:	Open the Share charm
Windows key + I:	Open the Settings charm
Windows key + K:	Open the Devices charm
Windows key + O:	Lock the screen orientation
Windows key + Q:	Open the Search charm to search everywhere or within an open app
Windows key + S:	Open the Search charm to search Windows and the web
Windows key + W:	Open the Search charm to search Settings
Windows key + Z:	Show the commands available in the application
Windows key + space-bar:	Switch input language and keyboard layout
Windows key + Ctrl + space-bar:	Change to a previously selected input
Windows key + Tab:	Cycle through recently used desktop applications
Windows key + Ctrl + Tab:	Cycle through recently used Windows 8.1 apps
Windows key + Shift + Tab:	Cycle through recently used applications (except desktop applications) in reverse order
Windows key + Left/Right key:	Snap an application to the left or right side of the screen.
Windows key + full stop (.):	Cycle through open applications
Esc:	Stop or exit the current task

TOUCH GESTURES

If you're using a touch screen Windows 8.1 PC, there's even more you can do. The Windows display is full of hot corners and hidden menus, which you can swipe and reveal to work faster and more efficiently.

Select Or Perform An Action

Just tap any item to launch it. On a Windows 8.1 touch-screen device your finger becomes your mouse, so in the classic Windows desktop, you need to double-tap while single-tapping will do in the new-look Windows.

App-Specific Commands

To get extra commands and options for the current app you're using, or just in the Windows Start screen, swipe up from the bottom of the screen.

Get More Options

Press and hold on the screen for three seconds to see the context menu.

Scroll Through Windows

Whether you're using Internet Explorer or just looking through apps on the Start screen, just place your finger on the screen and move it up, down, left or right to move the page.

Drag And Move

You can drag items around in Windows 8.1 by pressing and holding on an item to select it and then moving your finger around the screen (still holding down) to reposition it.

Find Recently Used Apps

To see apps you've been working on, slide your finger in from the left-hand edge of the screen and then slide it back to the edge again. You can then select the app by tapping the thumbnail.

Close An Application

Press and hold the screen at the top edge and then drag the window to the bottom to close it.

Above: To close an application, drag the app to the bottom of the screen – the window will shrink and disappear.

Zoom In And Out

Pinch your fingers together on the screen to zoom in and separate them to zoom out.

Access The Charms Bar

Swipe your finger in from the right-hand edge to reveal the Charms bar, with options for searching, sharing, devices and settings.

Turn And Pivot Items

Hold two fingers on an item you want to rotate and twist them in a circular motion.

Switch Between Apps

To quickly switch back to the last item you were working on, swipe your finger in from the left-hand side.

Arrange Apps

You can have apps displayed half-screen or even quarter-screen by tapping and holding the top of the screen and then dragging it to the left or the right. To make it even smaller, keep hold of the app and move it to the far side of the screen until it snaps into a new position.

Above: To arrange the windows side by side, drag their title bars to the required side of the screen.

SECURE YOUR PC

When you first get started with your Windows PC, getting it secure is vital. Unfortunately, a sad fact of modern computing is that the Internet is filled with nasty things that are designed to harm your computer or worse, steal your private information in an attempt to defraud you. It may sound extreme, but that's the reality of the dangers faced every time you surf the web. However, it's easy to stay secure and there are tools built into Windows 8.1, and even more freely available on the Internet to help you stay safe.

Above: A green bar and tick mean Defender is running as it should.

WINDOWS DEFENDER

Windows Defender is Microsoft's anti-malware protection built into Windows 8.1. It should run by default, but sometimes it can be overridden by the pre-installed trials that are shipped with new PCs by retailers. In previous versions of Windows, Defender was just a back-up program that tackled a specific type of threat. However, it's been beefed up in Windows 8.1 to cover all types of security threat.

What Is Malware?

Malware is a type of malicious program that can take many forms. There are viruses, which can cause damage to your PC, and spyware, which collects information about you and sends it back to its creator. While less well-known and publicized than viruses, spyware can be much more damaging.

Malware can infect your PC in many forms. All too often, software you might innocently download might be infected, so running anti-spyware software is extremely important.

PROTECT YOUR PC WITH WINDOWS DEFENDER

First, it's important to check that Windows Defender is turned on and working properly. In the Windows 8.1 Start screen, just type 'defender' and then choose the program from the results.

Windows Defender uses a traffic-light system to tell you what's going on. If the top bar is green and there's a tick on the computer screen graphic, then all is well. If there's another colour, there's work to do.

Check The Status

To see if Windows Defender is on and functioning properly, there are two status lines in the main screen. The first says Real-time protection, which should say 'On', and the second is Virus and spyware definitions, which should say 'Up to date'.

Left: Turn on Defender to protect your computer.

If either of those two statuses say anything different, you'll need to take action. A button will be placed in the main window for you to turn protection on or off. After that, the status of Windows Defender should show your PC as protected and turn from red to green.

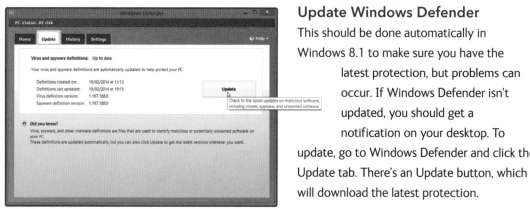

Above: You can update Windows Defender manually by clicking on the Update tab, then the Update button.

Above: Once a scan is underway, a coloured bar will indicate how far the scan has progressed.

Update Windows Defender

This should be done automatically in Windows 8.1 to make sure you have the latest protection, but problems can occur. If Windows Defender isn't updated, you should get a notification on your desktop. To update, go to Windows Defender and click the Update tab. There's an Update button, which will download the latest protection.

Run A Scan

Windows Defender also has the ability to scan your PC for spyware, as well as just stopping it from installing in the first place. To run a scan of your PC, look at the right of the Windows Defender pane, where you'll see a box with scanning options.

The first is a quick scan, which only looks in critical folders on your PC. The second is a full scan, which will take time searching every file on your computer, looking for any suspect files. The final option is a custom scan, where you can specify a folder for you to check, which is useful if you have a particular suspicion.

PROTECT YOUR PC WITH A SECURE LOGIN

One of the biggest threats to your PC, aside from malware, is theft, and this is particularly important for people who use a Windows 8.1 laptop or tablet. If someone steals your PC, they can gain access to all your private files and a host of information, so it's essential to secure your PC.

Stop Unauthorized Access To Your Files

The first thing to do is make sure you use a Microsoft ID. This means that when your PC is turned off or in sleep mode, a password is required to log in. If you're not

> **Hot Tip**
> Swapping numbers for similar letters is a great way to make your password secure. Try swapping an @ symbol for an a and a 3 for an e. Using upper-case letters also adds an extra level of security.

Above: Once you have a Microsoft account, you can set up (and change) a password to prevent unauthorized access to your files.

already using a Microsoft account to access your PC, you can set it up by going to Settings in the Charms bar, Accounts and then Use a Microsoft account. Set a password and your PC will be secure.

Use A Picture Password

If you don't want to use a complex password to secure your PC, Windows 8.1 offers an alternative called Picture Password. This uses a photo of your choosing, which you set up with invisible hotspots.

To set up your Picture Password:

1. Swipe in from the right edge of the screen, tap Settings, then tap Change PC settings, or if you're using a mouse, point to the bottom-right corner of the screen, move the mouse pointer up, click Settings, then click Change PC settings. Tap or click Accounts, and choose Sign-in options.

Above: Confirm your picture and crop, then you will be asked to create three gestures on your picture, which will be the password.

2. Under Picture Password, tap or click Add. Click Choose picture to select a photo for your sign-in. You can browse your Pictures library for suitable shots. Windows 8.1 doesn't offer any shots for you, so if you don't have anything suitable, you will need to find something from the web and add it to your Pictures folder.

3. You now need to draw three patterns on the screen. As you draw one, the highlighted number on the left will change. You can draw a shape, a line or just tap the screen. Remember what you do, and in which order. When you've drawn all three, repeat the process. Press Finish and your Picture Password will be applied.

Hot Tip

It can be difficult to log in using a Picture Password, so use a range of gestures. It's much better to choose an image that has sentimental value, so you can set up points on the image that you'll remember.

BACK UP WINDOWS 8.1

Disaster can strike at any time and, in seconds, whole digital lives can be erased due to hardware crashes, disk failures or, in rare cases, malware infections. It can happen to anyone, and it doesn't matter whether you have a budget system or an expensive Ultrabook, a Mac or a PC, new or old. Luckily, Windows 8.1 makes it easy to protect your files from digital disaster.

WHAT DO YOU NEED TO BACK UP?

It's highly advisable to invest in external storage for backing up your system. Many people use a partition on their hard drive, which virtually creates a second storage area on the same physical disk. This is obviously unwise, because if the disk fails it will take down all partitions.

Below: This Buffalo portable hard drive can hold up 1 TB of data.

External Hard Drive

To back up safely, it's best to invest in an external hard drive, which plugs into your PC via the USB port. It's the simplest way to store your backups, and you can pick up large-capacity drives relatively cheaply, with 1 TB systems (1000 GB) available for around £60.

Network Hard Drive

If you have multiple PCs at home, a network hard drive could be your best backup solution. The premise is the same as the external hard drive, but the drive plugs into your router, so it can be used by all computers on your home network.

Hot Tip

Solid-state hard drives are much more expensive than normal drives, but they don't suffer the same fallibility when it comes to debilitating crashes. They're worth considering for the extra peace of mind they'll give you, and they're much faster than your average spinning disk drive.

Cloud Storage

Online storage, known as cloud storage, has grown hugely in the last few years, and with home broadband speeds improving, backing up your system over the Internet is now a viable solution. You get 7 GB of storage with OneDrive, which helps, but there's more available for a fee. However, services such as Carbonite and Livedrive are also worth investigating. The benefit of cloud storage is that in the event of fire or flood, your backup drives won't be affected.

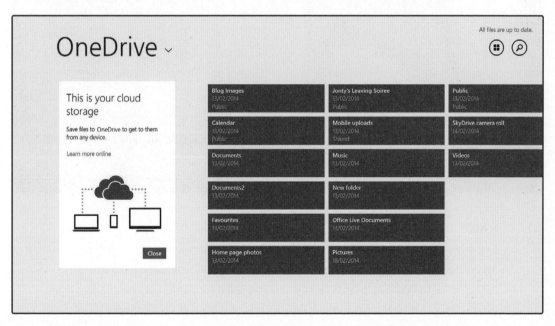

Above: Online storage services such as OneDrive offer a way of storing your files in the cloud, making them accessible anywhere.

RAID

Extremely diligent people use a system called RAID to back up their PCs, which ensures against failure of the backup drive. People have had their PC crash and gone to their backup drive to find that, over time, that disk has failed too. RAID uses two backup drives which mirror their data, effectively making a copy of a copy. It's rather tricky to set up, costly and not suitable for everyone.

WAYS TO BACK UP IN WINDOWS 8.1

There are many ways to back up your Windows 8.1 system and keep your files safe.
Each method offers slightly different benefits, but the good news is that you can use them
all simultaneously for ultimate peace of mind.

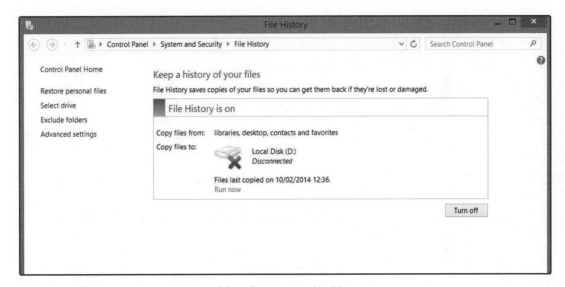

Above: Turn on File History in order to save a back up of all your files to an external hard drive.

Hot Tip

File History is an extremely
powerful backup tool and will
make copies of your files to an
external drive every 10 minutes if
you choose. You can tweak the
frequency in the Advanced menu.

FILE HISTORY

File History is a new back-up tool within Windows
8.1, which makes it easy to back up your system to
whichever media you choose.

Start Backups In File History

When you plug a drive in for the first time,
Windows 8.1 will ask if you want to configure
the drive for use with

File History – Windows' backup tool. Tap or click the option, and opt to switch on File History.

If this option doesn't appear, just search File History from the Start screen. When you turn on File History, it will back up all your libraries, which are the Documents, Music, Photos and Videos folders on that device.

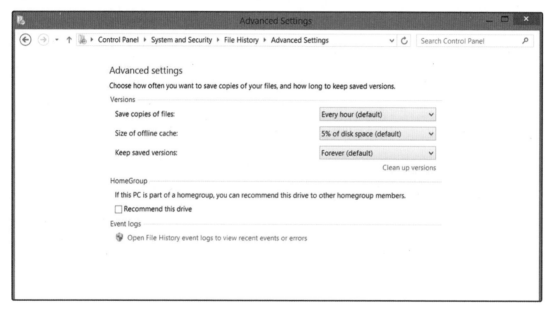

Left: Use the Advanced Settings in File History to tweak the frequency of backups and control allotted temporary backup space.

Fine-Tune File History

If you select the Advanced Settings function in the File History, you can change the following options:

- **Save copies of files:** The frequency with which your system backs up to the external drive. Choosing every 10 minutes will mean that, in the event of disaster, file loss is minimal.

○ **Size of offline cache**: If you ever disconnect
your drive, Windows 8.1 will start a temporary
backup on the drive, which will be uploaded
to the disk when you plug it back in. This
determines how much of your disk space is
given to that temporary backup.

○ **Keep saved versions**: Every time a file is
saved, a version will be kept by File History.
That's great while you're working on it but, over
time, the need for legacy versions diminishes.
You can change the length of time here.

Hot Tip

File History takes up a lot of
room. However, in Advanced
Settings, go to Clean Up
Versions. This enables you
to clean up backups over a
certain age, which keeps the
size of your backups in check
and will return valuable
hard-disk space.

USE SYSTEM IMAGE BACKUP

The System Image feature enables you to take a snapshot of your entire system and save it to an external drive. If the worst were to happen, you could resurrect this image on a new system and have everything back the way it was before.

At the bottom of the File History screen is the option to create a System Image backup. It's best set up once your PC is working perfectly and, in the event of a disaster, is then used to recreate your system and reload your files from the File History backup. *See* page 224 for how to restore your PC using a System Image.

Above: Choose where to store your system backup (System Image): on an external hard drive, DVDs or on a network.

SYSTEM RESTORE

While you use your PC, Windows 8.1 automatically takes snapshots of your system to use as a Restore Point – the feature is on by default. If you suffer a PC crash, you can go back to a point when your PC worked well. It's a great way of overcoming serious problems, but your files won't be up to date, and if your hard drive fails, these backups will be lost too.

Hot Tip

It's advisable to create a System Image in partnership with, rather than instead, of a File History. While a system image might seem more comprehensive, the tool can't keep up the pace of creating a new image every time your files change. However, it's still the fastest way to resurrect your system if the worst should happen.

ALL ABOUT APPS

INTRODUCTION TO APPS

One of the biggest changes that Windows 8.1 has brought to users is apps, something that was once the preserve of tablet and smartphone users. However, the power of apps can now be enjoyed by any user of Microsoft's latest operating system.

WORKING WITH APPS

Apps are all the rage, these days, and you'll find them on tablets, smartphones, TVs and even the latest smartwatches. Therefore, it's inevitable that Window 8.1 will make the most of them too.

Above: A view of apps arranged helpfully on the Start screen.

What Are Apps?

Apps are small programs that help you get things done. They tend to do specific jobs and there's no one type of app. Unlike traditional Windows programs that you buy in stores, apps are small, lightweight and often free, yet their simplicity makes them easy to use, enabling you to dip in and out at will, getting much more from your computing experience.

Apps are usually operating-system specific, so there are dedicated ones for Windows 8.1 in the same way Apple has apps for its iPhone and iPad devices. Apps for iPad, for example, can't be used on Windows 8, although you'll often see the same titles appearing in the respective app stores.

Where Do You Download Them?

Every operating system has a marketplace for apps, where you can browse and download the selection. In Windows 8.1, this is the Windows Store, which you can access from the Start screen. The Windows Store is a one-stop shop for every Windows 8.1 app, and free and paid-for apps are thrown in together for you to browse.

Above: The distinctive shopping basket logo for the Windows Store makes the button easily visible on the Start screen.

The Default Apps

You'll meet apps as soon as you log into Windows 8.1 for the first time, and the new Start screen is home to a host of included options. The Email, Photos and People apps are among the plethora of included titles to help you get started.

Hot Tip

There's also an online store for the apps in Windows. Just go to http://windows.microsoft.com/en-gb/windows-8/apps to browse the selection from any Windows PC. They're only compatible with Windows 8, however.

THE STOCK WINDOWS APPS EXPLAINED

As we explained, Windows 8.1 is packed with a host of apps as soon as you turn your PC on for the first time. Here's what they do.

Above: You can easily copy over any files, such as photos, to the cloud with OneDrive.

ONEDRIVE

Many of Windows 8.1's unique and best features come from its cloud integration, which means how much of its information it draws from the web, rather than that stored on your hard drive. OneDrive is the key part of this 'cloud' storage, and you get 7 GB of storage for documents and photos on the web.

Hot Tip

You can find OneDrive listed alongside your libraries and other hard disks in the Windows File Explorer. This means you can use it like any other physical drive.

READING LIST

One of the hidden gems included with Windows 8.1, this app stores articles you enjoy online, and saves them to be read when you're away from an Internet connection. When reading any web page online, just access the Share charm and choose the Reading List app from the list.

SKYPE

Sign In To Chat

One of the world's leading video messaging apps has been built into Windows 8.1, making the operating system the perfect place to chat to family and friends. If you've signed in with a Windows account, there's no need to sign in again, and you'll see existing contacts displayed in the main window. Long-time users of Windows will be surprised about how many existing Skype contacts they have, but newbies will see a blank screen ready to connect to people.

Add Contacts

Skype will find existing contacts from your old contacts in Hotmail, MSN Messenger and other programs, but adding new people is easy. Click or tap the Search button at the top of the screen and then type the screen name, email address or even name of a user before tapping on Search Directory. When they appear in the list, just choose Add to Contacts. A user must accept your invitation before you can chat.

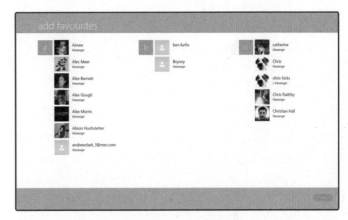

Above: Add the contacts you call or message most often to Favorites.

Start A Video Call

When a contact is online, you'll see a green dot next to their profile, showing that they're ready to chat.

Above: The phone icon starts a voice call; the camera icon a video call.

If there's no dot, they're not online, while orange or yellow mean 'busy' and 'away' respectively. To start chatting, just tap an online contact, and you can Instant Message each other in the right-hand window. To start a voice call or video call, tap the camera and telephone icon on the left.

BING WEATHER

More than just your bog-standard rain-checker, the Weather app is one of the best-looking we've seen. The interface is well laid out, giving you short-term and long-range forecasts, overlaid on gorgeous backgrounds.

Hot Tip

Look out for Bing Weather's app tile on the Windows 8.1 Start screen. It's a 'live' tile, so when connected to the Internet, it will show you the weather without the need to access the app at all.

BING NEWS

This news app uses Microsoft's search engine Bing to give you a roundup of the latest headlines. You can swipe through the news like a giant newspaper and, when you click on a story, it's easy to read and clearly laid out. Like the weather app, the tile will cycle through the headlines, so you can stay up to date without launching the app.

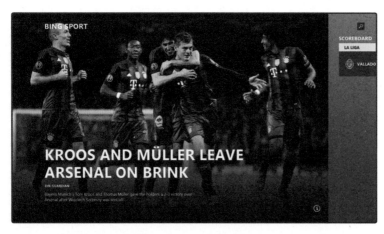

Above: Keep up with all key sports news with Bing Sports.

BING SPORTS

With headlines pushed on to the Windows 8.1 Start screen, sports fans are well catered for with this well-laid-out app. However, you'll find more than just Bing among its sources, with content brought in from the likes of *The Independent*, the Press Association and Sky Sports. It's a great way to keep up with the news and benefits from a breadth of sources.

BING TRAVEL

Packed with city guides and photos from over 2,000 destinations, Bing Travel is a fantastic app for those who love to travel. There are also areas for finding flights and hotels, with information pulled from the web, making it easy to plan trips without trawling the web.

Above: From transport to accommodation, Bing Travel helps you find everything you need.

BING FINANCE

If you love to keep up with the markets, this finance app is on hand to give you live updates straight to the Windows 8.1 Start screen. As well as general information on the FTSE and Dow Jones, you can watch your own portfolio too.

Hot Tip

The Bing Finance app also has a currency converter built in. Just access the Options menu by swiping from the bottom or right-clicking. As it's connected to the web, all exchange rates will be current.

BING MAPS

Explore The Map

Bing Maps is one of the best in the business and puts the world at your fingertips. You can navigate around the globe using your mouse – or touch screen if you've got a tablet or hybrid – and pinch and zoom into areas of the map.

Check The Traffic

That's not all, however: you can get live traffic information and routes, so you can check your route before you set out. Press the space-bar, choose Map Style and then hit Show Traffic, and watch as the roads on your map turn to coloured routes, using a traffic-light system to warn of delays.

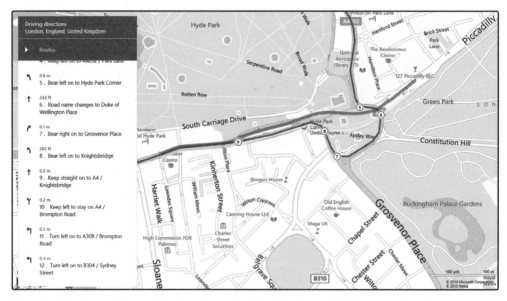

Above: Bing Maps shows traffic hotspots by colour-coding roads, and provides directions, highlighting your route on the map.

Get Local Information

Bing Maps can also help you find out more about what's around you. Just tap space (or swipe from the bottom of a touch-screen PC) to bring up the Options menu and hit Search. A new panel will appear on the right with options for food, sights, shops, hotels and more.

Hot Tip

You can also use the search function to find specific local attractions. Once located, there are options to visit the business's website, or get directions from your current location.

PHOTOS APP

The place for viewing photos on your Windows 8.1 PC, Photos can do more than the traditional applications that come with Windows. As well as letting you view the snaps on your hard drive, Photos enables you to connect to OneDrive (previously known as SkyDrive) to see your photos too.

EDITING YOUR SNAPS

A new feature brought in to Windows 8.1 was the ability to edit your pictures from within the Photos app. To make an edit, view the image full screen and then click or tap anywhere on your picture. There are quick options to rotate or crop your image at the bottom, in case it's the wrong way round, or if you believe it could benefit from being trimmed into a specific area.

Above: The Photos app offers various advanced editing options and previews of changes made.

Advanced Editing

If your editing needs are more advanced than a simple crop, then the

Hot Tip

If you want to improve your snaps without the hassle, then Autofix is your friend. Just make sure the option is selected on the left and then tap the panels on the right to check out possible changes. Every tile you tap will preview the effect in the main window, with the top item being the original.

Photos app can help you here too. Bring up the options menu again by clicking on the photo and then press Edit in the bottom right corner, and the view will change to have more edits on the left, and previews on the right.

Basic Fixes

Tap this option and the right panel will change, and show the same rotate and crop options you'll recognize from the main screen. In addition, you'll see options for red-eye removal and retouch. Tap the Red eye option and then click the offending pupil to have the colour banished. The Retouch option works the same way, but clones out blemishes, making it easy to subtly remove spots, or crudely erase photo-bombers.

Light

This option lets you control the brightness, contrast, highlights and shadows in your photos. To apply the changes, just click and hold your mouse on the option, or tap with your finger on touch-screen devices, then just drag outwards to increase or decrease the light in the photo. The changes will be previewed.

Hot Tip

If you don't like the effects you've added to your photos, don't worry. Just press Ctrl + Z to undo the last change, and keep pressing to go right back to the beginning.

Colour

This option enables you to change the temperature (how warm the colours are), add tints, change the saturation of the colours and enhance the colours in your photos. The first three options require you to press and hold (then drag your finger to turn the dial) to change the levels, while Color Enhance requires you to select the option, tap or click on the area you want to enhance and then use the white arrow to change the levels in that area.

Effects

The last two effects are two of the best in the Photo app; the ability to add a vignette and the addition of a focus point to your images. A vignette is a vintage-style darkening of

Above: To adjust colour temperature, click the button and turn the dial in the required direction.

the corners, which you can control after holding your mouse or finger on the option. The selective focus option puts a box on the screen, which you can drag to place and resize. Everything outside that circle will be blurred, while everything inside it will stay crisp.

CAMERA

Not one for desktop or even laptop users, but if your Windows 8.1 tablet has a camera, this app will handle the snapping. It's packed with features, which enable you to change the quality of your pictures as well as setting timers for selfies. See page 212 for a full guide to the camera.

PEOPLE APP

More than just your standard contacts app, the People app in Windows 8.1 brings together everyone from your email and social networks into one place, and helps you keep up with what they're doing.

Above: Browse contacts using the A–Z tabs on the home screen.

EXPLORING CONTACTS

You can search for specific contacts using the search bar in the top right, or browse using the A–Z tabs on the home screen. If you notice that you have multiple entries for people, just click their profiles and choose Link contacts. You can then add any duplicate profiles and have them combined into one.

GET UP TO DATE

The What's New tab enables you to get updates from their social networks so you can see everything in one place. You can access the tabs by right-clicking to get the options menu, after which you get options to

Above: What's New updates you on contacts' social media activity.

see your own profile, all contacts and, of course, what's new. A timeline of updates from your contacts will appear, with updates from Twitter, Facebook, LinkedIn, Outlook and more.

ADD SOCIAL MEDIA

Of course, it's a great contacts app as well, and you can search your contacts using the alphabetical tabs on the right and then choose how you'd like to contact them. As you'd expect, the app works well with Skype, and means you have email, video calling, Twitter and Facebook to call on.

Hot Tip

If you see that a social network isn't appearing in your list, you can click the Connected To link in the bottom right followed by Add an account. Choose the service from the list and then log in using your details.

Above: The People App brings together the multitude of ways you can contact your friends and family in one place.

XBOX APPS

There are three Xbox apps that come as part of the Windows 8.1 package. Here, we give you an overview of what you can do with the Games, Music and Video apps; we go into more detail on all of them in Chapter 5.

XBOX GAMES

Windows 8.1 and the Xbox are built to work together, but even if you don't have a Microsoft console, there's still plenty on offer here. Games have become a huge part of the Windows 8.1 apps offering, and the Games app can track achievements and progress.

Above: The Xbox Games app enables you to edit gaming profiles and show achievements and much more.

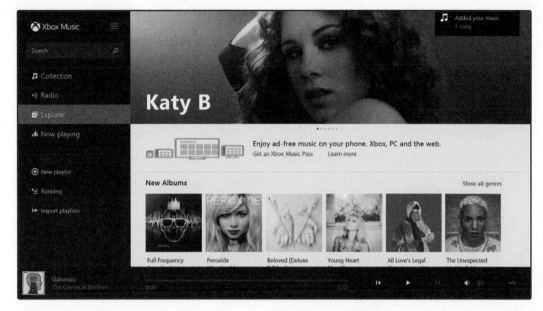

Above: Xbox Music enables you to play music from your personal collection, buy songs and stream millions of songs for free.

XBOX MUSIC

In Windows 8.1, you don't have to rely on your MP3s for your music collection. Streaming – the act of subscribing to a service and listening to any music you want over the Internet – is a great way to enjoy music. To see more on using Xbox Music, turn to page 180.

XBOX VIDEO

Windows 8.1 also has its own built-in video service, which enables you to rent and buy movies to watch on your device. To access the Xbox Video service, just tap or click the Video tile. Turn to page 200 to find out how to get the most from it.

Hot Tip

The Health and Fitness app is a new addition to Windows 8.1. You can use it to track exercise and keep track of your daily calorie count, as well as reading aggregated content from various sources about the latest ways to keep in shape.

MAIL APP

The Mail app has been given a good overhaul in Windows 8.1 to make it one of the most powerful email clients around. Built with touch-screen devices in mind, but equally good for traditional mouse and keyboard users, it's clearly laid out, well designed and powerful. You can run multiple email accounts simultaneously, making it perfect for home and business users alike.

SET UP YOUR EMAIL

If you've signed in with your Windows ID, the Mail app will open with your email already present. The Mail app is completely open, so it doesn't matter if you have

Above: The Mail app is clearly laid out, with certain types of emails being handily filed away separately.

a Microsoft-based Hotmail or Outlook address, or a Gmail. Whichever email you've used for your Windows ID will be found as soon as you open the app.

Add Other Accounts

When you open the app for the first time, Windows should prompt you to add any other accounts you have. It's not unusual to have more than one email address, and you can have as many as you like in the Mail app.

If Windows doesn't prompt you to add another account, it's still easy to set up multiple email addresses.

1. Open the Mail app from the Windows 8.1 Start screen.

2. Bring up the Charms bar by swiping from the edge or placing the mouse pointer in the bottom-right corner and choosing Settings.

3. Tap or click Accounts.

4. Tap or click Add an account, choose the type of account you want to add, then add your username and password.

Most accounts can be added with only your username and password. In some cases, you'll be asked for more details, which you can usually find on your email account's website.

USING THE MAIL APP

Select Multiple Messages

Swipe from left to right across each message (in the middle pane), or right-click on each message that you want to select. To select a group of continuous messages, hold down the Shift key and then press the up arrow or down arrow key.

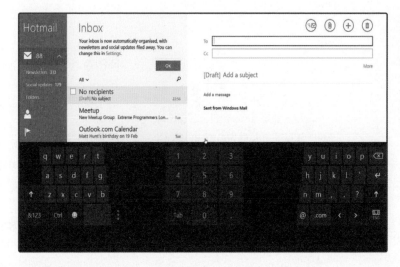

Above: To create a new message, tap or click the '+' icon at the top and tap or click the 'To' field in order to type in the recipient's name or email address.

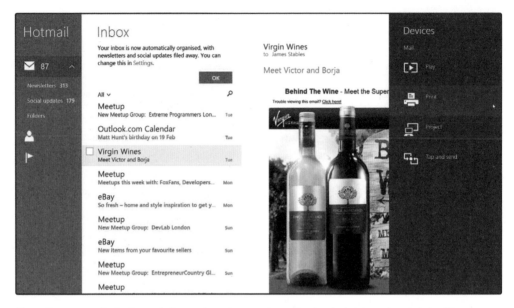

Above: To print an email, select Print in the Devices charm, choose a printer and settings (such as page orientation), then Print.

Hot Tip

You can add an email signature, which is displayed automatically at the end of your messages. To create one, just open the Settings charm, tap or click Accounts, and choose the correct email account. Find the Use a signature option and write your sign-off.

Reply, Reply All, Or Forward

Tap or click the Reply icon in the upper-right corner, which has an envelope with a looping arrow.

Delete Messages

Select one of more messages and then tap or click the Trash icon in the upper-right corner.

Search For Messages

You can quickly find text or someone's name from an email message by tapping or clicking the Search icon or simply begin typing in the Mail app.

Print A Message

Select an email message, then open the
Devices charm, tap or click Print, choose
a printer, then choose Print.

Send Attachments

In a new email message, tap or click the
paperclip icon in the top-right corner.
Select the file you want to add to the
message and then tap or click Attach.
You can also attach multiple files.

Mark Messages As Read/Unread

Select one or more messages, then swipe
down from the top of the screen and
choose Flag, Junk or Mark as unread.

Create Folders And
Move Messages

Swipe down from the top of the screen,
then tap or click Folder options to create
a new folder, or Move to move the
selected messages.

Add A Contact

Tap or click an email address from an
email to create a new entry in the
People app. Tap or click the Save icon
in the top-right corner.

CALENDAR APP

The Calendar app in Windows 8.1 is more limited than its Mail counterpart. You can only use Outlook and Microsoft Exchange calendars; Google's popular service is not supported. However, it's still an excellent app with plenty of great options.

MASTER YOUR CALENDAR'S VIEWS

The Windows 8.1 Calendar app has a host of views, which enable you to clearly see your up-and-coming appointments, dates and events. You can switch between them by accessing the Options menu; to access this, swipe from the bottom or right-click in the main window.

Above: You can sync your Facebook or Outlook account to your Calendar in order to see contacts' birthdays.

Add Appointments

You can add items to your calendar by accessing the Options menu again, and then choosing New. You'll then see a new window, where you can add a title, date, time and location. You can also add notes and information.

Show More

Click or tap the Show more link to get even more options for your calendar entry. You can add attendees for your event, if they're in your People app. You can also set handy reminders, and the drop-down menu enables you to set an alarm to alert you before the start of an event.

Hot Tip

In the Options menu, you can see upcoming appointments by choosing What's Next. The Day option will show you a plan of that day's events, and there are also options to view all events scheduled for the rest of the week and month.

DOWNLOAD APPS

As well as the apps that come as standard with Windows 8.1 that we have just described, there is a whole world of apps waiting for you to download in the Windows Store, on every possible topic.

GET STARTED WITH THE WINDOWS STORE

All apps are found within the Windows Store, which is available on all Windows 8.1 devices. You can find the link on your Start screen, indicated by the shopping bag on the green tile.

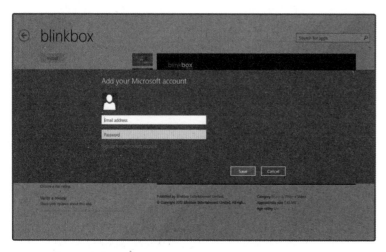

Above: Before downloading any new apps, you need to sign into the Windows store.

Signing In

To download apps from the Windows Store, you need a Windows account, which you should have set up when logging into Windows for the first time. Enter your username and password at the first screen, or if you're running without one, go back to page 66 to find out how to set up an account.

Introducing The Store

Once you've entered the Windows Store, you'll be presented with a series of tiles. If you've still to upgrade to Windows 8.1 (from Windows 8), then this will be the first one you see. Turn to page 64 to see how to install it for the first time.

Above: Once logged into the Windows Store, you will see a highlighted app – i.e. a suggestion of one you might like.

The first thing you'll see is a highlighted app, which is hand-picked by Microsoft as being worthy of your attention. Just keep scrolling to the right using the mouse, tapping the right and left arrow on your keyboard, or by swiping on a touch screen.

Browsing The Store

You'll notice that the apps disappear at the right-hand side of the screen, and the page scrolls right through a list of app categories. There's Social for networking apps such as Facebook and Twitter, Entertainment for TV and movies, and of course Games, which is one of Windows 8.1's most popular and vibrant sections.

Hot Tip

After the first Spotlight section, you'll see apps picked by manufacturers such as Samsung, Sony or Lenovo. Many of these apps will be exclusive to you, and not enjoyed by the wider Windows 8.1 population. No matter which brand your PC is, the manufacturers' picks will sit second in the list and, while the quality here will be lower than that of the general Windows Store, it's worth taking a look.

There are 25 sections altogether, from the fantastic Games section to the less alluring Government, so there's truly something for everyone. Just click a category and you'll be delivered to a new window, again with an easy-to-browse view.

Searching The Store

The search box is located in the top right, and it's easy to type what you're looking for. Just tap into the box, start typing and the results will appear as you type, narrowing with every stroke. When you see your app appear, just tap or click it to be taken to its page.

Hot Tip

Each category has a sub-section for new, top paid, top free and a selection of sub-categories. Just tap or click any of these headings to get even more choice, making it easy to find the apps you want.

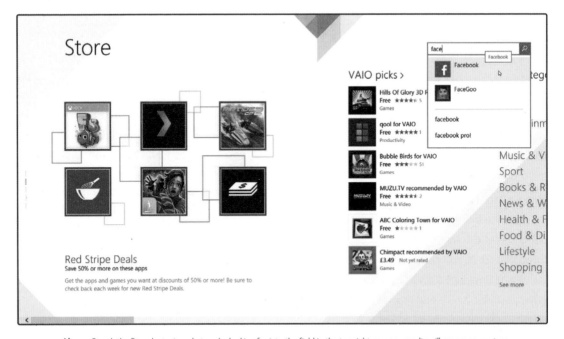

Above: Search the Store by typing what you're looking for into the field in the top right corner – results will appear as you type.

Free Apps

The Windows Store is a mixture of free and paid-for apps, but no one really likes forking out when they don't have to. Handily, the Windows Store has a category to let you browse free apps on the main page, and every category has its own free library too, so you can weed out the deals.

Paid-for Apps

In the main, paid-for apps are better quality than the free ones, for obvious reasons, so if you're looking for the best choices, filtering out the ones that cost can be a wise move. As with free apps, you can see the paid-for ones on the home screen, and in each app category.

BUYING APPS

Before splashing out on an app, it's well worth checking you're buying a quality product. There are refund options available through the Windows Store, but it can be time-consuming, so preventing mistakes is recommended.

Hot Tip

When you click on an app, you can see reviews and recommendations from past users, which can give you a clue about whether that particular app is worth the cash. Scroll right and you'll see a rating out of five. This is the average of all app ratings, so the higher the number, the better the consensus of opinion.

Read The Comments

If you scroll even further to the right, you can read comments from app users, which should give you more information. If you're satisfied, you're ready to download your app.

Right: Check out reviews of apps before you commit your hard-earned cash (as refunds can be a hassle).

How To Download An App

Free apps will simply have an Install button in the left-hand pane, while paid-for ones will have Buy. To install an app, just tap the button and a notification will appear in the top right-hand corner to let you know that the app is installing. Clicking or tapping this will show the download's progress.

Above: You don't have to enter payment details to download a free app, but it might be handy if you expect to buy apps.

Hot Tip

When your app has finished downloading, it will automatically be installed and added to the Start screen. If you can't see it, swipe or drag down on the home screen and look in the alphabetical list. Any newly installed apps will be marked 'new'.

Buying Paid-For Apps

When you press Buy, you'll be asked to confirm your account's password before being whisked off to the payment page. You'll need to enter card details, which will be saved for next time.

MANAGING YOUR PAYMENTS

Manage Payments On Your Windows Store Account

On the Start screen, tap or click Store to open the Windows Store. Swipe down from the top edge of the screen, then tap Your account. Tap or click Add payment method or Edit payment method, edit any necessary info, then tap or click Submit.

Remove A Payment Method From Your Account

1. On the Start screen, tap or click Store to open the Windows Store.

2. Swipe down from the top edge of the screen, then tap Your account. (If you're using a mouse, right-click, then click Your account.)

3. Tap or click Remove.

4. Sign in to the billing website with your Microsoft account.

5. Tap or click Payment options.

6. Choose a payment method, then tap or click Remove.

Above: It's easy to add or edit payment details for the Windows Store in the Your account section.

HOW TO USE APPS

Once you've downloaded your apps, the fun has only just begun. As you'd imagine with the eminently customizable Windows 8.1, there are many ways to get more from apps, from organizing them to work more efficiently to multitasking for the ultimate Windows experience.

MASTER YOUR APPS

Once you've downloaded your apps, getting the most out of them is key to your Windows 8.1 experience. Those who use their apps to their fullest potential will soon realize how powerful a tool Windows 8.1 can be.

Above: You can organize and customize the Start screen to have your apps set up your way.

Find An App

To access an app in Windows 8.1, just scroll through the Start screen. This is fully customizable, so to get an alphabetical list of apps installed, just swipe down on the Start screen or click the down arrow that appears in the bottom left-hand corner. Just tap or click any app tile or list item to open the app.

Hot Tip

Every app has a set of custom options that you can access in a number of ways. Specific app options can be accessed by swiping up from the bottom of the screen or right-clicking anywhere on the screen.

Share From Within An App

Many Windows apps have sharing options built in. To share elements via social media, email or other services, just access the Charms bar by swiping in from the right-hand edge or placing your mouse in the bottom right-hand corner. Choose Share and the available options will be listed.

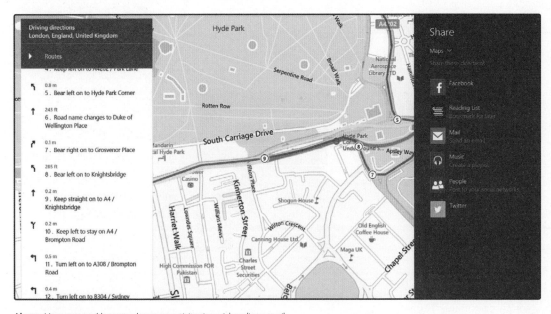

Above: Many apps enable you to share your activity via social media or email.

Above: App multitasking lets you view, say, your email at the same time as photos.

Hot Tip

When you resize an app, the display will change to accommodate its new shape. That means you can keep your email to just a quarter of your screen and still see your inbox clearly.

App Multitasking

The best thing about Windows 8.1 apps is that you can run up to four on the screen at any one time. Just drag the top of your app – either with your finger or the mouse – to either side of the screen to snap it into place, then just load another and it will sit in the vacant space. You can then resize it by dragging the black bar.

Above: Switch between apps by swiping previous apps out from the left-hand edge.

Switch Between Apps

To switch between apps, just swipe in from the left-hand edge and you'll switch back to the last app you were using. Do it again and you'll summon the app before that. Keyboard and mouse users don't miss out, however, and placing the mouse pointer in the top-left corner will show a preview of the app, and clicking will make it full screen.

See All Apps

You can also see a list of all running apps. On a touchs-creen device swipe in from the left (as if switching apps), then slide back to the edge again; with a mouse, put the pointer in the top-left corner and then move it down the left-hand edge. Each app that's open will be previewed as a thumbnail. If you're using a mouse, place it in the top-left corner and then move the mouse down the far left-hand edge to see the same list.

Close An App

If you want to close down your app, click or tap and hold at the top of the app screen and drag down to the bottom. The app will disappear into a small square, which just needs to be dragged to the bottom of the screen.

Upgrade Your Apps

Most apps will update automatically – which is the default setting for Windows 8.1 – but you can check for new versions by summoning the Charms bar, choosing Settings > Update and Recovery and looking for updates to install.

Delete Your Apps

If you're fed up with an app or want to regain some hard disk-space, you can quickly and easily delete apps. Tap and hold an app and the Options bar will appear at the bottom. To get rid of an app, just tap or click Uninstall.

ORGANIZE YOUR START SCREEN

Prevent your Start screen from turning into the Wild West by organizing your apps; try banishing rarely used icons or increasing an app's size and prominence so you can find what you need.

Pin Apps To The Start Screen

1. On the Start screen, slide up from the middle of the screen to see the Apps view. (If you're using a mouse, click the arrow button near the lower-left corner of the screen.)

2. Press and hold or right-click to select the apps you want to pin.

> **Hot Tip**
>
> On the Start screen, press and hold the tile you want to move. If you're using a mouse, click and hold the tile. Drag it around the screen and the app tiles will move around it, as it snaps into position.

3. Tap or click Pin to Start. The apps you pinned will appear at the end of your Start screen.

Above: Choose favourite apps to pin to your Start screen to make them even more accessible.

Resize An App

Tap and hold to bring up the Options bar and choose Resize. You can then choose how much space the tile takes up on your Start screen. Regularly used apps should be made larger and be easier to spot, while lesser-used apps are better left much smaller.

Above: It is easy to arrange your apps in logical groups and give the groups names to make them super easy to find.

To Create A Group Of Tiles

On the Start screen, press and hold or right-click the tiles you want to group together. Drag them to an open space and when a grey bar appears behind them, release the tiles. This will create a new group. If you want to name the group, tap or click where it says Name group and enter a new name.

Move A Group Of Tiles

On the Start screen, pinch to zoom out. (If you're using a mouse, click the Zoom icon in the lower-right corner of your screen.) Press and drag or click and drag the group of tiles you want to move to where you want it to go. Once you're done moving groups, tap or click anywhere on the screen to zoom back in.

GETTING CONNECTED

INTRODUCTION TO THE WORLD WIDE WEB

Nearly every new wonder that your Windows 8.1 PC enables comes via the Internet, and the web continues to change and shape our lives. Not only is your PC, tablet or phone now constantly connected, so are elements of the home too, with TVs, stereos and even kettles now controlled online. Windows 8.1 is the most connected version of Microsoft's OS to date, so if you're ready to see all that it's capable of, it's time to connect to the world wide web.

WEB JARGON EXPLAINED

The number of abbreviations and terms can make the world of the web seem as though it has its own language. Let us translate for you.

Airplane Mode

A setting where all connections are disabled. When travelling on aircraft, you are only permitted to use tablets and laptops that are turned to Airplane Mode. In Windows 8.1, you can access this in PC Settings.

Browser

This is the program on your PC that enables you to view web pages and surf the web. There are many brands of browser, with Internet Explorer being the default for Windows 8.1.

Cloud

The catch-all name given for services that live on the web. OneDrive, Dropbox and Hotmail are all examples of cloud services.

Download

Any information transferred from the Internet and saved locally to your PC has been downloaded.

Encryption

This is a method of protecting data by turning it into an unbreakable code. You can encrypt files so they're unreadable to anyone else. There are apps that can encrypt files on your PC such as TrueCrypt (www.truecrypt.org), or online cloud services such as Mega (https://mega.co.nz).

Ethernet

This is the standard type of cable for connecting networked devices. Most PCs have this type of connection, but as Wi-Fi becomes ubiquitous, this method of physical connection is being phased out on modern PCs to enable lighter designs.

Above: Ethernet cables are being replaced by Wi-Fi as the most common way to connect your computer or tablet to the internet.

HomeGroup

This is the name for the managed network of Windows 8.1, Windows 8 and Windows 7 devices in the home, as well as devices such as printers. The HomeGroup works out some of the more complicated aspects of creating a network, to enable you to link PCs quickly and securely.

IP Address

This is the unique long number that serves as your device's identity on your network and the Internet in general. On your network, each device will have a number that looks like this – 192.168.0.X.

ISP

This is your Internet Service Provider, the company that provides your connection to the web. Like British Gas or any other utility company, they connect your home to their network, piping the Internet in. Without them, you wouldn't get a connection.

Malware

Any virus, spyware or small malicious app designed to do damage to your PC or steal information from you. Malware is common and you need a good antivirus program to deal with it. Windows Defender, included in Windows 8.1, is designed to prevent malware, but there are other paid-for packages on the market with more features, such as Norton, BitDefender or Kaspersky.

Mobile Broadband

Unlike broadband that uses your phone line to connect, mobile broadband uses the 3G and 4G networks, predominantly used by mobile phones. Connections are sometimes slower and less reliable, depending on your nearest mobile masts, but good reception and a 4G connection can offer better-than-ADSL speeds.

Modem

A modem (meaning modulation and demodulation) is the gateway between your home network and the Internet. It deciphers the web into a format your PC can understand, and does the same for information from your PC which is heading out on to the web. Most routers supplied by ISPs have a modem built in, but many off-the-shelf routers do not, which means they'll have to be plugged into a router in order to access the Internet.

NAS

Network Attached Storage (NAS) is the name for any storage drive that attaches to your PC across the home network. This enables you to access files from multiple PCs in the home and creates a safe way to back up your files.

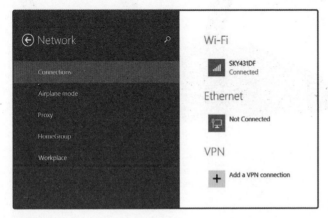

Above: Windows' Network Connections pane.

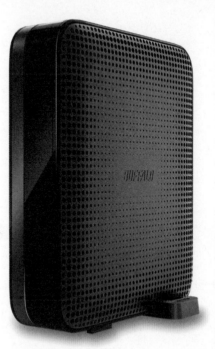

Above: A Network Attached Storage device, such as this, allows multiple users access to files.

Network

A network is the name for a collection of PCs, printers or other devices linked together. In the home, this group is linked by your router to become a Local Area Network (LAN).

Network Adaptor

This is the device that makes the connection between your PC and the router. Most laptops and tablets will have a wireless network adaptor build in, but many desktops don't, which means you'll need to buy one separately to connect to a Wi-Fi network.

Phishing

This is the name given to a style of Internet fraud, where perpetrators disguise fake pages as legitimate banking or social media services to skim off log-in details.

Router

This is the device that distributes your Internet connection to devices around the home. The router manages the connection to your PC, phone, tablet or any connected device, making sure each one can access the web.

Security Key

The password used for accessing a network. It's important to set up a password for your own Wi-Fi, so that people can't access it without your knowledge. Not only is accessing your network a crime, but you would be liable for anything they did while on it.

Above: Routers, such as the one pictured here, provide wireless Internet access to any connected devices in your home.

Spam

This is unsolicited email, which can often spread malware. Most email applications have antispam filters built in to catch mail it thinks is unwanted. Just as annoying as real-life junk mail, spam can have a sinister side: it is the key way in which harmful phishing attacks are spread.

Proxy

This is another type of connection, where your location is hidden, or broadcast as somewhere else. Firstly, this provides a more secure way of connecting to the web, but it's also widely used to connect to services that aren't available in your location.

Upload

This is the process of information leaving your devices or network and being loaded on to the Internet.

URL

This is the unique address for a website. The address www.bbc.co.uk is a URL.

WPA2

This is a type of Wi-Fi password that's stronger than the older WPA or WEP standard. When setting up a network, look out for this option, which will make your home Wi-Fi more secure.

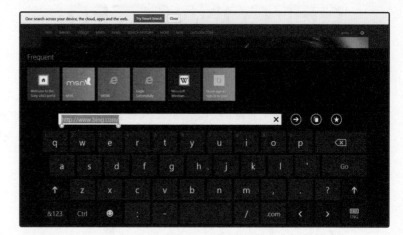

Above: When you type a URL (uniform resource locator) into your browser, it will provide you with a link so you can connect straight through to a particular website.

VPN

Virtual Private Network is a type of connection used to connect remotely to secure, private networks.

Wi-Fi/Wireless

Wireless, more commonly called Wi-Fi, is the method of connecting to a network without plugging in.

Wired

This is the description of any device that is connected to a network by an Ethernet cable.

WPS

Wi-Fi Protected Setup is a type of Wi-Fi connection that enables you to press a button on your router and chosen device, rather than using passwords typed into Windows 8.1. WPS isn't on every device, but it makes for an easy way of connecting laptops, printers and devices to routers.

GET CONNECTED TO THE INTERNET

If you already have an Internet connection set up, it's just a case of getting your new Windows 8.1 PC connected. But if you're setting up your broadband connection for the first time, then you'll need the right hardware to connect. Here's what you need.

WHAT DO YOU NEED TO CONNECT TO THE INTERNET?

- A subscription to an ISP's broadband service.
- A modem router (supplied by your ISP).
- A PC that has a network adaptor (every modern PC will have this).
- A network (Ethernet) cable.

FOR WIRELESS CONNECTIVITY

- A wireless modem router (every modern router will have this).
- PC with a wireless card (all laptops and tablets will have this, but check desktop PCs).

Hot Tip

Having trouble getting a wireless signal throughout the house? Try investing in a powerline system, which uses two plugs to send the Internet around your home through your plug sockets.

CONNECT TO THE INTERNET VIA ETHERNET

After you've signed up to an ISP and you've connected your hardware by following the ISP's instructions, you should be ready to connect to the Internet. Just plug an Ethernet cable into the back of the router and then into your Windows 8.1 PC.

CONNECT TO A WI-FI NETWORK

You can connect to a network by swiping in from the right edge of the screen, tapping Settings, then choosing Network. You'll then see an option for Wi-Fi, which you need to click or tap. Choose the network you want to connect to, then tap or click Connect. If you're unsure of the name, it's often written on the side of your supplied router, along with the password. Enter the network security key and password, or username if you're asked to do so, and then click OK.

Above: To connect to a Wi-Fi network, go to Settings/Network, and choose from the networks listed there.

CONNECT VIA WPS (WI-FI PROTECTED SETUP)

If your router has a WPS button, you can connect without the hassle of passwords and log-ins. Turn on the PC and once at the Windows Start screen, connect to a network by swiping in from the right edge of the screen, tapping Settings and going to PC Settings and choosing the network from the list. Instead of typing a security key or password, press the Wi-Fi Protected Setup (WPS) button on the router. The router will connect the PC to the network and apply the network's security settings automatically.

Hot Tip

With newer routers, this password-free setup can also be called Windows Connect Now (WCN), so check to see if your equipment has this handy feature.

KEEP YOUR DATA PRIVATE

The beauty of using a Windows laptop or tablet is that you can connect to the Internet while you're away from home. Whether it's in a café, pub, hotel lobby or a friend's house, it's easy to get online and do everything you need wherever you are.

However, public Wi-Fi hotspots can be insecure, and unscrupulous hosts can use the network not only to see what you're doing, but to gain backdoor access to your PC. That doesn't mean you shouldn't use public Wi-Fi. It means you should be vigilant and use the fantastic public network settings in Windows 8.1.

⊖ BTWiFi-with-FON

Find devices and content

Find PCs, devices and content on this network and automatically connect to devices like printers and TVs. Turn this off for public networks to help keep your stuff safe.

Off ▋▃▃

Properties

SSID:	SKY431DF
Protocol:	802.11g
Security type:	WPA2-Personal
IPv6 address:	fd36:109b:8ba6:0:d0a8:3b05:38b7:9e67
IPv4 address:	10.234.173.27
IPv4 DNS Servers:	192.168.22.22
	192.168.22.23
Manufacturer:	Intel Corporation
Description:	Intel(R) Centrino(R) Advanced-N 6235
Driver version:	15.10.3.2
Physical address:	C4-85-08-EA-C8-EC

Copy

Left: Protect data: turn the Find devices and content settings off.

Public Network Protection

When you've completed these steps, you'll still be able to access the web, but you'll be safe from anyone else on the network who might want to snoop on your files and information.

Hot Tip

If you connect to a network and receive a warning about its security certificate, it means there's no encryption. This means everything you do can be read by the host of the network, so if you do use it, don't type any passwords or login details.

1. Swipe in from the right edge of the screen, then tap Settings. If you're using a mouse, point to the bottom-right corner of the screen, move the mouse pointer up, then click Settings and choose PC Settings from the bottom right-hand corner.

2. Tap or click Network, tap or click Connections, and then find the name of the network you want to connect to.

3. Turn off Find devices and content, which is found at the top of the list. Now other devices also on a public network won't be able to see your files. However, remember to switch it on again when you get home.

BROWSE THE WEB WITH INTERNET EXPLORER

Internet Explorer is the default browser in Windows 8.1, which is your gateway to surfing the web on your PC. There are actually two versions of Internet Explorer installed on your PC: the desktop version with which any previous user will be familiar is Internet Explorer 11, and a touch-friendly version which is built into the Start screen. It's still very powerful, but easier for those using tablets and hybrid PCs. However, some web pages don't open well, so if you have problems, click or tap the bottom bar, hit the spanner icon and choose View in the desktop.

THE MODERN UI INTERNET EXPLORER

The touch-friendly version of Internet Explorer can be accessed using the tile on the Start screen, and it opens a full-screen version of the browser. The bar for entering web addresses appears at the bottom and, like its full-screen counterpart, it acts as an entry point for URLs and search terms alike. As you start to type, IE will suggest sites you might be looking for, which you can tap and click.

Left: IE is Windows' default browser, available as both touch and non-touch versions.

Bookmark A Website

Swipe up from the bottom edge, or click the bar to bring up the app commands. Choose the Favorites button, which is represented by a star with a plus. Tap the star icon next to the URL bar to access previously stored bookmarks.

Above: Access Modern UI Internet Explorer through the tile on the Start screen.

InPrivate Browsing

If you don't want other PC users to see the sites you've been using, or are worried about leaving your accounts logged in accidentally, you can use the InPrivate feature. You browse as normal, but things like passwords, search history and web-page history are deleted when you close the browser. To start browsing InPrivate, swipe up from the bottom edge (or right-click), choose the Tab tools button and then New InPrivate tab.

Above: Bookmark a site by tapping or clicking the Favorites button, depicted as a star with a '+'.

Hot Tip

Internet Explorer for the Modern UI has a Flip Ahead feature, which predicts the page you're going to click on next. Tap or click the arrow on the right to access the next page. You can turn it on by going to Settings > Internet Options > Flip Ahead.

Above: Make it easy to access a favourite site by pinning it as a tile to your Start screen.

Hot Tip
If you're using a touch-screen device, you can easily browse backwards and forwards through pages by just swiping left and right.

Pin A Site To Your Start Screen

You can pin sites you use all the time as tiles to your Start screen. To pin a site, swipe up from (or click) the bottom edge to bring up the app commands. Tap or click the Favorites button, tap or click the Pin site button and then tap or click Pin to Start.

Save Pages To A Reading List

When you come across an article or other content that you'd like to read later, you can add it to a reading list in Internet Explorer. Access the Share charm and then choose Reading List to have it added. Reading List is a separate app in Windows 8.1, which you can access by searching 'reading' on the Start screen.

Above: Come back and browse it later by adding it to your Reading List.

INTERNET EXPLORER 11 (DESKTOP)

The desktop version of Internet Explorer is more traditional, and much better suited to those using desktop PCs and large-screen laptops. The address bar is at the top, and again doubles as a search box. This version of Internet Explorer benefits from add-ons and is compatible with most web pages.

Above: The desktop version of Internet Explorer is better for larger screens.

Change Default Search Provider

In this version of Internet Explorer, you can set your own search provider. To do so, tap the settings cog on the taskbar and choose Internet Options followed by Manage.

Download Files

To download a file, just click the link on a web page. Internet Explorer will ask you if you want to download it and will give you two options: 'Run' will download the file and open it straight away, while 'Save' will add it to your downloads library or other specified location.

> # Hot Tip
> You can add a site to your Start screen in the desktop version of Internet Explorer; just tap the settings cog on the taskbar and choose Add site to apps.

Use Add-ons

Add-ons are small apps that sit within Internet Explorer and help you get more done. They're only available in the desktop version. As above, go to the Manage add-ons menu and choose Find more toolbars and extensions at the bottom of the menu.

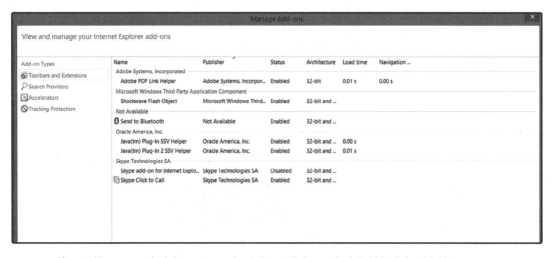

Above: Add-ons are apps that help you get more done in Internet Explorer, and include Adobe Flash and Quicktime.

Above: If you add a site to the Tracking Protections List, information about your browsing activity there cannot be collected.

Add Bookmarks

When you're on a site you'd like to bookmark, just tap the star icon on the toolbar. The Favorites menu will pop up. Choose Add to favorites. All your bookmarks will be available in the menu beneath, under the Favorites tab.

InPrivate Browsing

Again, if you want to hide your web history and logins you can. Just head to the cog icon on the taskbar, choose Safety and then InPrivate browsing. There's also an option here to switch on Tracking Protection. This stops advertisers from reading your browsing history.

Hot Tip

If you use a desktop PC, you may want to stop links opening in the Modern UI version of Internet Explorer. To do this, just search 'internet options' on the Start screen and, in the Programs tab, choose Always in Internet Explorer on the desktop.

NETWORK YOUR PCs

Most people have more than one PC in the home, and it can be frustrating when one PC has a file on its hard drive, but you're using another machine. That's where networking comes in. Networking means linking your PCs together in your home so they act as one giant machine. You can share your data across all PCs, as well as things such as external storage and printers. Sound good? Well, the good news is that Windows 8.1 makes it easy to set up.

WINDOWS HOMEGROUP

A HomeGroup is Windows 8.1's name for a group of PCs on a home network that can share files and printers. HomeGroup is available in Windows 8.1, Windows RT 8.1 and Windows 7. If your other PCs are using other operating systems, you can still network them, but you won't be able to use Windows 8.1's tools to do it.

Above: Having a HomeGroup makes it easy to share files.

What Can A HomeGroup Do?

Using a HomeGroup makes sharing easier. You can share pictures, music, videos, documents and printers with other people and devices in your HomeGroup.

You can help protect your HomeGroup with a password, which you can change at any time. Other people can't change the files that you share unless you give them permission to do so.

After you create or join a HomeGroup, you select the folders and locations on your Windows 8.1 PC (for example, My Pictures or My Documents) that you want to share. You can prevent specific files or folders from being shared, and you can share additional libraries later.

Creating A HomeGroup

When you set up a PC with Windows 8.1 or Windows RT 8.1, a HomeGroup is created automatically on the first PC. It's then up to you to add other devices to the group. However, if you clicked to disable sharing when you first set up Windows, you will need to re-enable it.

1. To access the settings, first open HomeGroup by swiping in from the right edge of the screen, tapping Settings, PC Settings, and then tap or click Network followed by HomeGroup.

2. In the HomeGroup menu, tap or click Create. Select the libraries and devices that you want to share with the HomeGroup. You can opt to not share things like movies, videos or pictures, for example, but to allow documents.

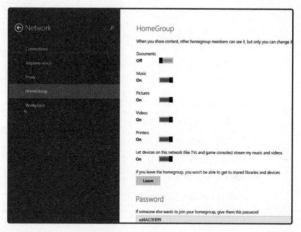

Above: When setting up a HomeGroup, select what will be shared.

Above: Activate Find devices and content for HomeGroup to work.

You can also use games consoles, such as the ubiquitous Xbox 360, to play content stored on your PCs. Tap or click the Media devices option if you want to allow these devices on your HomeGroup.

Adding Your Other PCs To The HomeGroup

There's no point in setting up a HomeGroup with one PC, so log on to your next PC running Windows 7, Windows 8.1 or Windows RT 8.1 and join your new group.

You'll need the HomeGroup password, which you can get from any HomeGroup member. All user accounts, except the Guest account, will belong to the HomeGroup. It will be up to that user how much they share or withhold from their own account.

1. Find the HomeGroup password on the original PC by going to the items in the Settings. To do this, swipe in from the right edge of the screen, tap Settings, PC Settings, and then tap or click Network followed by HomeGroup. The password will be displayed at the bottom of the screen.

2. Go to the PC you want joined to the network, open the HomeGroup menu again, enter the HomeGroup password and then tap or click Join.

3. Enter the HomeGroup password, then tap or click Join.

4. Select the libraries and devices that you want this PC to have access to.

Finding HomeGroup Files

The beauty of files shared via HomeGroup is that they will appear in your own PC's File Explorer, as if they were on your own drive. However, for you to see other PCs on your network, they must be awake, connected to the network, have their sharing switched on, be members of the HomeGroup and have their libraries shared. Once you've confirmed all this, you're ready to go.

To access shared libraries on other HomeGroup PCs, open This PC by swiping in from the right edge of the screen, tapping Search and entering This PC in the search box and choosing this option from the list. Under HomeGroup, tap or click the libraries you want to access. You'll now see a list of files. Double-tap or double-click the files or folders you want.

Sharing Libraries

When you create or join a HomeGroup, you select the libraries and devices you want to share with other people in the HomeGroup. Libraries are initially shared

Above: All files in the HomeGroup can be seen in File Explorer.

Above: You may choose not to share all your files with others.

with read-only access, which means that other people can look at or listen to what's in the library, but they can't change those files. You can adjust the level of access at any time, and you can exclude specific files and folders from being shared.

Share Individual Files

To share individual files or folders, search for 'This PC' on the Start screen and choose it from

the list. Select the item, then tap or click the Share tab, which is located on the toolbar in Windows Explorer.

There are different Share with options available, depending on whether your PC is connected to a network and what kind of network it is. To share items with a particular user, choose that person's account from the list.

You can opt to share a file with everyone in the HomeGroup by choosing this option from the list. You'll notice two HomeGroup entries and in brackets next to the name, you'll see the rights those users will have. If you want them to be able to edit the files, then choose the option with 'view and edit.' If you don't want them to make changes, just tap the one with 'view'.

Above: To share a file, tap the Share tab and select a share option.

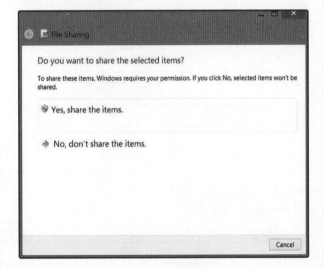

Above: Click No, don't share the items to prevent others sharing.

Hot Tip

To prevent a file or folder from being shared with anyone, tap or click the Share tab, then tap or click Stop sharing. This will make it disappear from anyone's view who's not using your login.

ADVANCED SHARING

Sharing in Windows 8.1 is almost unrivalled, but you won't want to share everything with everyone. You may not want everyone to read your private documents, but you might want a family member to be able to input into the itinerary for a holiday or maybe help with homework. Luckily, it's easy to change permissions as you go.

CHANGE PERMISSIONS

If you have files or folders you want to share in specific ways, then it's worth checking out the advanced sharing option in Windows Explorer. You can access it by clicking once on any file or folder and then clicking the Sharing tab on the toolbar, which runs across the top of the window.

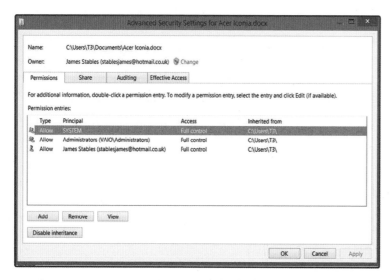

Above: The Permissions settings enable you to allow or deny specific users access to particular files or folders; to set this up, click the file or folder, then the Share tab.

The Permissions box lists everyone who has access to the file, and what level of control they have over it. You will see that the system has control, which is best left as it is, that all administrators have access (that could be other profiles if they're set up with administrator privileges) and your own username. If you want to upgrade or downgrade the privileges of your users, *see* page 166.

You can add users to this list by clicking Add and then clicking or tapping Principal user and typing their name into the box and pressing Check name. When the name comes up, press OK. You can then choose the type of access they have. If they're already added, but you want to change their access, just single-click their name and choose Edit.

SHARING A PRINTER

If you have a printer that's connected to a PC in your home using a USB cable, you can share it with your HomeGroup. Networking your printer using a Windows 8.1 HomeGroup is much simpler than setting up a normal network printer, although the downside is that you'll have to have it physically connected to your PC.

Hot Tip

The PC that your printer is connected to must be on, or other devices won't be able to print.

1. To share your printer, open HomeGroup by swiping in from the right edge of the screen.

2. Tap or click the control to Share printers and devices.

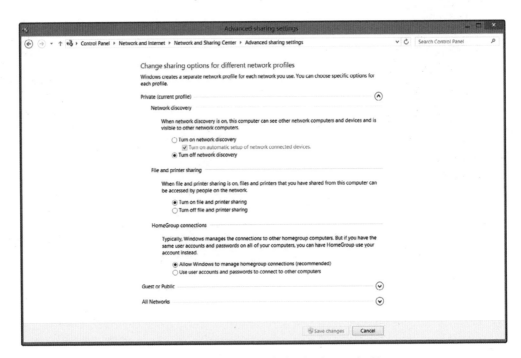

Above: The Turn on file and printer sharing option must be ticked in order for other devices to be able to print.

3. Once the printer has been shared, you will be able to see it on any PC in the HomeGroup. To print, just open the Print menu of the application you want to print from by hitting Ctrl + P, or click or tap File > Print.

CHANGE YOUR HOMEGROUP PASSWORD

The standard HomeGroup password is a random mix of numbers and letters, which can be hard to remember, especially when you're going around your devices setting them up, or adding a new one down the line. The good news is that you can change your password to something a little more memorable. Here's how:

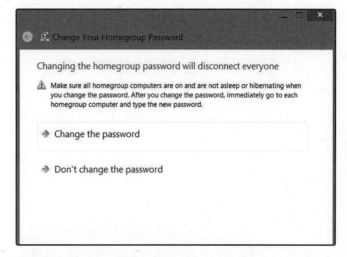

Above: Change your HomeGroup password to something memorable.

1. Head to the Control Panel by summoning the Settings charm while on the Windows 8.1 desktop.

2. Under the Network and Internet heading, click Choose HomeGroup and sharing options.

3. Tap or click Change HomeGroup password.

4. Tap or click Change the password. You might be asked for an admin password or to confirm your choice. Press OK when you're done.

Hot Tip

If you want to prevent a PC from being included in the HomeGroup, just go to the Settings menu and choose Change PC Settings. Click HomeGroup and then choose Leave.

SET UP A NETWORK HARD DRIVE

If you have multiple PCs in your home, it's possible to back them all up to a single hard drive. What you need is a network hard drive. It's a normal storage device that plugs into your router and can be used by any device in the home – PC, tablet or even smartphone.

WHAT'S A NETWORK HARD DRIVE?

Network Attached Storage (known as NAS) means you have a hard drive accessed over your home network, rather than directly connected to your PC. Unlike your computer's hard drive, which is inside your PC, a NAS drive connects to your home router.

Above: Having a network hard drive means that all files are backed up and can be accessed by everyone in the home.

WHY NETWORK YOUR HARD DRIVE?

The advantages of a networked drive are numerous, and using one is highly recommended. Firstly, it can be shared by any computer on your network, so all files are accessible to everyone in the home. NAS drives also make for a fantastic backup, because as they're separate from the PC, if a PC were to crash, corrupt or otherwise lose its data, the NAS drive would be unaffected.

Set Up Your Network Hard Drive

1. Connect your networked drive to your home router using the supplied Ethernet.

2. The drive will come with some installation software. These are all slightly different, so refer to your documentation regarding the exact set-up process here.

3. Once that stage is complete, it's time to find it in Windows 8.1. Type 'network' on the Start screen and choose the desired option from the results.

4. Find your drive in the list. If it hasn't appeared, there's been a problem with the installation, so check your documentation again.

5. To have your drive work as a normal attached hard drive, right-click or tap and hold This PC in the left-hand pane and choose Map Network Drive.

6. Choose a letter for your networked drive and then, in the browse box, choose it from the list of networked items.

Hot Tip

Some network drives enable you to access your files remotely. This means you can get to your files from anywhere in the world, without having to leave your PC running. Most NAS drives have this function built in.

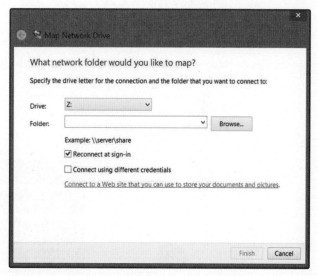

Above: When you map a network hard drive, you are creating a shortcut to it; during the setup process, you should assign it a letter.

7. Your network drive will now appear alongside your hard drive and any USB storage, and can be accessed by any PC on your network, as long as you repeat the set-up process for each device.

USE THE CLOUD WITH ONEDRIVE

In Windows 8.1, you get a whopping 7 GB of storage in OneDrive (previously called SkyDrive), Microsoft's own 'cloud' or web-storage service. This means you can access your files from any device in any Internet-connected location, so you don't need to carry your snaps around with you on a USB stick to show them off.

WHAT CAN YOU DO WITH ONEDRIVE?

In Windows 8.1, OneDrive acts like any other drive. You can share any file quickly and easily from within Windows Explorer, turning the web service into a drive that behaves like any other. To do this, just copy the file or folder you want to share to OneDrive, if you haven't already.

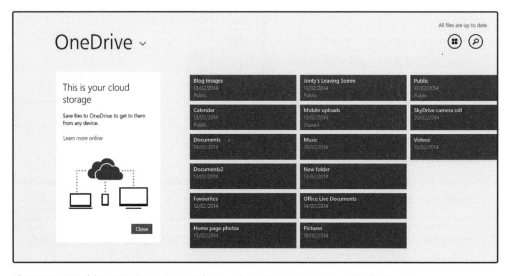

Above: Store 7 GB of data on OneDrive and access it from anywhere, as long as you're connected to the Internet.

To do this, open File Explorer, browse to the file or folder, and then drag it to OneDrive.

Share Your Files

When you save your files to OneDrive, you can also share them with other people by sending a link in an email, or getting a link that you can post on sites like Facebook, Twitter or LinkedIn, which means your friends don't even have to be OneDrive users to benefit. What's more, it can all be done from the Share charm.

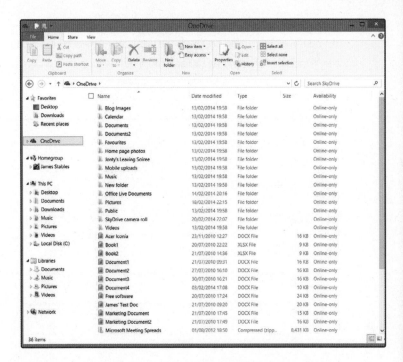

Above: Copy your files and folders to OneDrive, and you will be able to access them from wherever you are, making it convenient to work while on the go.

Add Files To OneDrive Using The App

On the Start screen, tap or click OneDrive to open the OneDrive app. You'll get an overview of all the files currently on your hard drive. If you want to add files by using the app, access the Options menu by right-clicking or swiping up from the bottom. Tap or click folders to browse to the location on OneDrive to which you want to add the files.

Hot Tip

You can email files directly from OneDrive. Just select the file, head to the Share charm and select Email from the list. It will be automatically attached, so you just have to type your message and press Send.

Save Files To Your PC

If you have files stored on OneDrive, you can view and download them to your hard drive using the Windows 8.1 app. Just tap any file and it will open in a compatible program. If you right-click or swipe on a file and select Make available offline, that file will be copied to your hard drive.

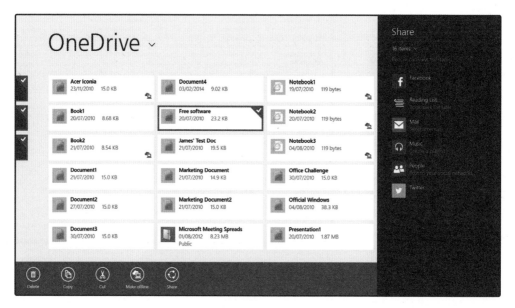

Above: OneDrive allows you to use the Share charm to share selected files with others via email, or as a link on Twitter or Facebook.

Automatically Saving Backup OneDrive

It's annoying when you don't have your files or photos when you need them most, which is why you can opt to have some kinds of files automatically saved to OneDrive. To set this up, swipe in from the right-hand edge of the screen, tap Settings, then tap Change PC Settings. For documents, tap or click OneDrive, and then switch on Save documents to OneDrive by default.

Hot Tip

If space on your PC isn't a concern, you can also make your entire OneDrive available offline. To make any file, or indeed your entire OneDrive, available offline, press and hold or right-click OneDrive in the left pane and then choose Make available offline.

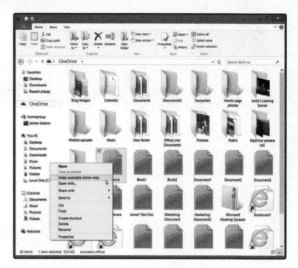

Above: As the contents of an online-only file are stored in OneDrive, it doesn't take up much of your disk space.

Access Microsoft Office Web Apps

OneDrive comes with web versions of all the Office apps such as Word, Excel and PowerPoint, which can be used to open documents, even if you don't have the paid-for software installed on your PC. The apps aren't as powerful as the desktop versions of Office, but they do have one benefit: you can share documents with friends and family, who can open, read and edit them regardless of the PC they're using or the software they have installed.

To access the Office web apps, you need to log into OneDrive using the web. In your browser, just go to onedrive.com and sign in with the same Microsoft ID you use for your Windows 8.1 PC.

Right: OneDrive's Office Web Apps make it possible for users to open Office documents, even if they don't have Office software.

MUSIC, VIDEO & PHOTOS

THE XBOX MUSIC APP

Your Windows PC is packed with ways to enjoy music, with not one but two dedicated apps for listening to your favourite tunes. Users of Windows XP and Windows 7 will be very familiar with the powerful Windows Media Player that comes with the operating system, and that returns here in Windows 8.1.

Above: The XBox Music app allows you to stream music as well as manage your own.

Hot Tip

Before signing up to a music-streaming service, there is one thing to be aware of. While you are paying your subscription you can listen to anything you want on demand, but if you let your subscription lapse, you'll have no access to any of the music and be left with nothing.

LISTENING TO MUSIC IN WINDOWS 8.1

In Windows 8.1, there's more provision for music than ever before. Taking pride of place on the Windows 8.1 Start screen is the all-new music app Xbox Music. More than just a media player, the app is part of Microsoft's huge new streaming service, which has over 30 million songs available online.

Stream Music In Windows 8.1

Music streaming is a new way to enjoy music, and the beauty is that you don't have to buy tracks or rip them to your PC. A music-streaming service enables you to listen to them from the Internet, and you pay a monthly fee rather than per song.

In Windows 8.1, the Xbox Music app costs £8.99/$9.99 per month, for which you get to listen to an unlimited number of the 30 million songs in its catalogue. Not bad when you consider that, on most download sites, a single album costs roughly the same.

Above: As well as being a streaming service, Xbox Music also has a Store facility so that you can buy tracks or albums you have particularly enjoyed listening to.

GETTING STARTED WITH XBOX MUSIC

The Xbox Music app should take pride of place on your Windows 8.1 Start screen, but if you can't see it, just type 'music' in that same screen and then tap or click the app when it appears. If you have MP3s on your PC already, the app will automatically find the files, as long as they're in your Music library.

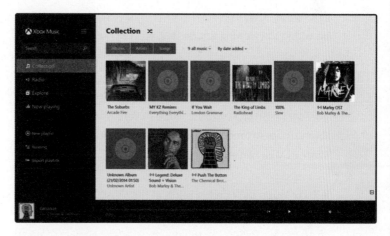

Above: The app enables you to organize your own music collection, whether the tracks have been purchased from iTunes or elsewhere, or ripped from CDs.

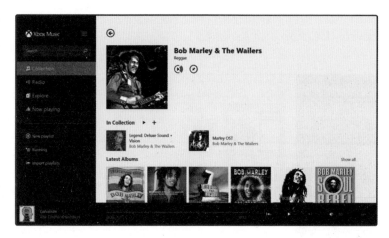

Above: If you choose to search your music collection using the Artist option, the Xbox app will list all the songs or albums related to that artist.

Find Your Music

If you have music in your library, then you can browse and listen to it using the Xbox Music app. When the app is open, tap the three-lines icon in the top left to open the Xbox Music menu. Tap or click the Collection option and the main pane will change to display all your music.

The top of the window has three buttons: Albums, Artists and Songs. Press one of these options and the music displayed on the screen will change to reflect that option. The menus will change to an alphabetical list within the viewing option that you've chosen.

Add Locations

It's up to you how you organize your music, and if you don't want to keep your MP3s in your Music library, it doesn't mean that you can't use Xbox Music as your player.

Hot Tip

If you have lots of music, you might find scrolling through the list of hundreds or even thousands of songs a little laborious. If you click or tap the '-' icon, it will reduce all entries to an A–Z list.

If Xbox Music can't detect MP3s in the Music library, it will let you add a separate folder. This is especially good for those who have used iTunes in the past, which whisks your music off to its own folder. Tap the option labelled 'we didn't find any music on this PC' and then choose the '+' icon. Browse to your folder of choice and press Add this folder to Music.

Play Your Music

To play, pause or skip a song from your collection, head to the Xbox Music app and go back to the Collection menu. Search for music using the Albums, Artists or Songs tabs; you can filter and sort by date, genre and name. Select a song or album and then hit the Play button on the bottom bar. Use the controls at the bottom of the screen to play, pause, skip and set other playback options.

Search For Music

Of course, you don't have to search for music manually. Just tap the search box and type the name of the artist, album or song you're looking for. The results will appear in the main window, with two buttons at the top. The option on the left will show music from your collection or in other words, music stored on your PC. The second is Full catalog, which is the music on the Xbox Music service. Unless you subscribe to the Music Pass, you'll only be able to listen to 30-second previews of these songs, so therefore it's best to look for music in the Catalog tab, which lists your MP3s.

Above: Music while you work? Entirely possible with Windows' app-snapping feature.

Multitask Your Music

If you want to listen to music while you use another app, it's easy using the snapping feature in Windows 8.1. Grab the top of the app and drag it to the left or right. When it snaps to half the screen, grab the three dots and resize the Xbox Music app to occupy a thin sliver at the far left or right of the screen, which enables you to work in a decent-sized window and still control the tunes. Use the playback controls in the smaller window.

Alternatively, you can open any app and keep music playing while you use the playback controls on your keyboard to control the playlist. When you want to get back to the Xbox Music app, just place the mouse in the top-left corner of the screen and move it down the list, or swipe in from the left and back out on a touch-screen device.

CREATE A PLAYLIST IN XBOX MUSIC

The Xbox Music app makes it easy to listen to music, and one way is to make lists of your favourite songs. Whether it's for a party, a night in, or for going running, you can group any bunch of songs together and create your perfect playlist.

1. In the left pane, choose New playlist, enter a name and then tap or click Save.

2. Now choose Collection, browse your songs, hit the '+' button and then choose the playlist name from the left-hand pane.

Above: The first step in creating a playlist is to give it an appropriate name.

Hot Tip

If you already have music set up in iTunes, you can move over all your playlists. Just tap the Import playlists option. Xbox Music will find and add them automatically.

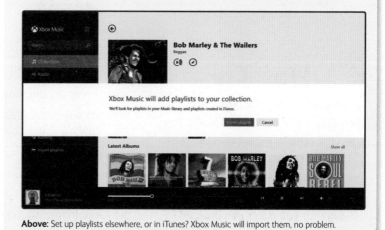

Above: Set up playlists elsewhere, or in iTunes? Xbox Music will import them, no problem.

3. Repeat until you have as many songs as you want in your playlist.

4. When you're done, find the playlist in the left pane and then tap or click the Play button.

5. To change the song order, press and hold one and drag to reposition it within the list.

Hot Tip

To remove a song from a playlist, select it with a single click or tap and hit the '–' button when it appears.

Above: Pressing the '+' button next to a song will add it to the playlist of your choice.

Hot Tip

To start a free trial, Xbox Music requires some payment details. The service renews automatically, so if you don't intend to start paying, make sure you make a note in your Calendar app to cancel it after 30 days, so you don't get charged.

START STREAMING IN XBOX MUSIC

While we've already shown you how to get the most from the music you already have on your hard drive, Xbox Music is capable of much more. As we mentioned, you can subscribe to the service to listen to a catalogue of over 30 million songs, putting an unimaginable amount of music at your fingertips. What's more, you get a month free, so there's no reason not to dive headfirst into the world of music streaming.

1. To start streaming music using the Xbox Music app, just load it up in Windows 8.1 and choose the Explore tab in the left-hand pane. At the top of the screen, you'll see a message that says 'Get an Xbox Music Pass'. Tap this link and some details about the service will appear. There's a box that says Free Music Pass Trial, which you need to tap.

2. Tap the free-trial option and you'll be asked to sign in using your Microsoft credentials.

3. Once that's sorted, add your credit card details. Press the Add a credit card icon, enter your details and click Confirm.

Stream Tunes In Xbox Music

When you return, the app will have completely changed. Instead of being only able to listen to full tracks from the music in your collection, you will now be able to choose from the full catalogue. You can browse through any album of any artist, choose any song and press play to hear it in full.

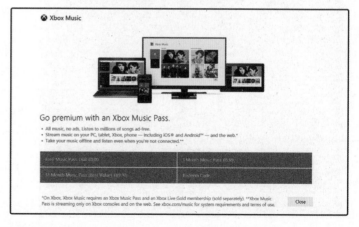

Above: Xbox Music lets you try before you buy (but only for 30 days though),

WINDOWS MEDIA PLAYER

While Xbox Music is an app that brings together streamed music and music stored offline on your PC, it can be frustrating for those who don't want to pay for a subscription service. The app tends to make it hard to browse without running into options to listen to 30-second previews. That's where Windows Media Player comes in. It's a much more powerful manager of offline music, and lets you listen to your MP3s, organize them, make playlists and much more besides.

INTRODUCING WINDOWS MEDIA PLAYER

Anyone familiar with previous versions of Windows will certainly recognize Windows Media Player. Unlike the Xbox Music app, it lives on the desktop rather than on the Start screen.

Above: The multitasking Windows Media Player is found on your desktop.

Open Windows Media Player

To open Windows Media Player, search for it on the Start screen. It's not pinned to the taskbar by default, so it's a good idea to do that the first time you access it, for easy access the next time. While it's open and on the taskbar, right-click (or click and hold) and choose Pin to Taskbar.

Find Your Media In Windows Media Player

When you start Windows Media Player for the first time, it will scan your libraries for all media files. You can find them through the Music, Video and Pictures options in the left-hand pane; just click or tap the option to display all your music in the main window, and double-click a song or video to play it.

However, if you still need to add a video or music track that's not in your libraries, it's easy. Go to any File Explorer folder and click the Organize tab on the taskbar, click Manage libraries and then choose Music or Video. A new box will open which shows the folders that Windows Media Player classifies as libraries. Press Add and navigate to any folder and choose Include folder.

Above: You can opt for the Player to search your Music library.

Above: You can change any folder into a Media library.

WATCH A DVD IN WINDOWS 8.1

To many people's surprise, the ability to watch a DVD on your Windows 8.1 PC was removed in the latest version of Windows, presumably in an attempt to get people to use the Xbox Video. That means if you're hankering to watch one of your DVDs on your Windows PC, you're in a spot of bother.

The best option is to download the free VLC Player from http://www.videolan.org. This powerful player can handle any kind of video file, and comes highly recommended. Just download and run the app, then insert a DVD into your optical drive. Open VLC and you will see your DVD in the left-hand pane.

CD AND DVD BURNING

Having a huge library of digital music on your PC is all well and good, but that won't do you much good in your car, or while you're away on holiday. However, you can create a CD that stores about 80 minutes of music, which you can use in normal CD players.

Burn An Audio CD

Enter Windows Media Player in the Search box, and then tap or click Windows Media Player. In the Player library, tap or click the Burn tab and choose the Burn options and select Audio CD. Search for songs that you want to burn to the disc and then drag them to the right-hand pane. This creates your 'burn list'. Insert a blank disc into your drive and, when you're ready, choose Start burn.

> ### Hot Tip
> You can make an MP3 (data) CD or DVD that can hold several hours of music, but it won't be readable in normal players, unless they have data capabilities.

> ### Hot Tip
> If you want to change the order of the items in the burn list, drag them up or down in the list.

Above: Burning a CD is only an option if your computer has a CD or DVD burner.

RIP CDS TO YOUR PC

One of the best features of Windows Media Player is its ability to turn your CDs into digital music files and store them on your PC. This process is known as ripping and it's perfectly legal as long as you own the CD in the first place.

Ripping CDs means you can have your entire music collection on your PC, so it can be played and enjoyed in more ways, not to mention backed up, so even if your original CDs get lost, destroyed or scratched, you still have your music.

When you rip music from a CD, you're copying songs from an audio CD to your PC. During the ripping process, Windows Media Player compresses each song and stores it on your drive as a Windows Media Audio (WMA), WAV or MP3 file.

1. Make sure your PC is connected to the Internet if you want Windows Media Player to automatically get info about the songs, such as the name of the CD, the artist and the titles of the tracks being ripped.

2. Open Windows Media Player.

3. Insert an audio CD into the PC's CD drive.

4. Tap or click the Rip CD button.

Left: Ripping your CDs is quick and easy with Player.

CHANGE THE RIP SETTINGS

When ripping music, there are all sorts of options you can select to make your music work your way, from the file format that Windows Media Player turns your CDs into, to where your files are organized and the quality of the music. To access the settings menu, just click the Organize tab and then click Options. Click the Rip Music tab.

Hot Tip

The top option in the Rip Music options menu is the location in which music is sent when you start ripping. The default location is the Music library in Windows 8.1, but if you want to have files stored in a different place, just choose Change.

Choose The File Format

The default file format for ripping CDs in Windows Media Player is Windows Media Audio (WMA), but that's actually not the best option. WMA isn't widely used or accepted, so if you rip all your files into this format, you may run into problems down the line. Click the drop-down menu and change this option to MP3. This is a universally recognized format and will work on any device.

Above: Use the options to alter your Rip settings.

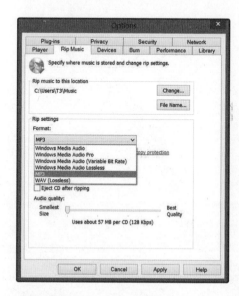

Above: MP3 files will work on all devices.

Above: The higher the bitrate, the better the sound, but the larger the resulting file, so decide which is the most important to you.

Change The Quality

The quality of digital music is measured by its bitrate, which determines how much information is held in the music file. The more information, the more detail and the higher the quality. Windows Media Player rips music at 128 kbps. Using the slider at the bottom of the window, you can up the quality from 128 kbps to 192 kbps. Be aware, however, that upping the quality makes the files larger, so if you have a small hard drive, you may not want to adjust it.

Add Album Information

If you're not careful when ripping CDs, you can turn a hard drive full of your best-loved songs into an indeterminate pile of unlabelled files. Windows Media Player identifies the names of the songs, the artists' names and the artwork via the Internet. If you rip when you're not connected, you'll get a lot of tracks titled 'Track001'; if the album is not found, you can do this manually.

Add Album Art Manually

If you do find yourself with unidentified albums, you can help Windows Media Player find the correct information. To find album artwork, open Windows Media Player and make sure you're in the library window. If you're not, click the Switch to Library button in the top-right corner.

In the library window, right-click any album that hasn't been identified and choose Find album info. Windows Media Player connects to the Internet and displays the Find album information dialog box. You can also find groups of albums by highlighting them all before completing the last step. To force the player to update the file, click Organize and then click Apply media information changes.

Above: The Player will search the Internet to locate missing album artwork.

Above: You can ask the Player to locate album info if it hasn't already done so.

SYNC MUSIC WITH A PHONE OR MP3 PLAYER

Listening to music on your PC is all well and good, but what about taking it away with you? You can use Windows Media Player to copy music, videos and photos from your Windows 8.1 device's library to a portable device, such as a smartphone or MP3 player. This is called synchronizing or syncing, and it makes carrying your music with you easy.

Which Devices Can You Sync With?

Windows Media Player's syncing capabilities may be synonymous with ageing MP3 players, but it's still a great way to keep your existing devices up to date. Windows Media Player can sync with devices such as Samsung Galaxy smartphones and tablets, and the popular HTC One. However, every phone is different.

Above: Sync Windows Media Player with your smartphone or tablet to make sure your entertainment is with you when you want it.

Start Syncing

First, connect your chosen device to your PC and switch it on. Open Windows Media Player, then either tap or click Finish to sync automatically, or tap or click Finish, then tap or click the Sync tab to choose files manually. If you want to customize the way the sync feature works, you can do that from within Windows Media Player. In the Player library, tap or click the Sync tab, then Sync options followed by Set up sync.

Above: To commence the syncing process, ensure your device is connected to your PC via a USB cable and is switched on.

STREAM TO OTHER DEVICES USING WINDOWS MEDIA PLAYER

You can also use Windows Media Player to stream content from your Windows 8.1 PC to other devices around the home. This could be to other PCs or games consoles such as the Xbox 360 or Xbox One. This means that if you have a movie stored on your PC, you can watch it in the comfort of your living room.

Above: The Stream tab's options enable you to stream media to your HomeGroup devices.

Start Streaming

1. Make sure that media streaming is enabled on your PC. To do this, just open Windows Media Player and make sure you're in the library window.

2. Click the Stream tab on the toolbar and choose Turn on media streaming with HomeGroup.

3. A new box will appear, which will list all the devices in your home. At this point, it's a good idea to go around your home and turn everything on, including smart TVs and games consoles. You might need to reopen Windows Media Player for them to be detected. Tick the Allowed box next to the devices you want to stream to, or hit the Allow All button, and press Next.

4. In the next window, you'll be asked which media you'd like to share. Make your selection by choosing Shared or Not Shared from the drop-down lists, and press Next. Make a note of the password and press Finish.

Sit Back And Enjoy

The types of media you shared should now be visible to other devices. The way you access will be different on every device: those with an Xbox 360, for example, just need to hit the Guide button, choose the Media blade and then the video player.

Each of your profiles will need to have sharing set up, so bear that in mind when choosing your device from the list. If you have multiple users on your Windows 8.1 PC, media streamers will pick up each one, so remember which account you've set up for sharing.

XBOX VIDEO

Like the Xbox Music app, Windows 8.1 comes with an app for video and it offers an attractive and easy way to get a host of entertainment on your PC. Of course, being a Windows 8.1 app, it's designed for touch screen, and you'll find it on your Start screen.

Above: Discover visual treats galore with the Xbox Video app.

WATCH MOVIES ON YOUR PC WITH XBOX VIDEO

Instead of the less touch-friendly Windows Media Player, you can use the Video app to watch all of the video content already on your PC. To watch it, just follow these steps:

Above: Click on or swipe the Open file icon to access a video.

Hot Tip

You can quickly open any video file by swiping up from the bottom, or by right-clicking and choosing Open file.

Hot Tip

To quickly search for a video, tap or click the search button in the top-right corner. Alternatively, you can tap or click videos, and then, using the arrow buttons next to videos and date added, you can sort and filter the list.

1. Open the Xbox Video app.

2. Slide or scroll to the left to see your personal videos.

3. Tap or click a video to play it.

4. If you want to pause a video, touch the screen or move the mouse, and then press Pause. You can also pause, change the volume and adjust other playback options by swiping up from the bottom of the screen or right-clicking anywhere on the screen.

Above: Access your own videos by opening the Video app and scrolling left.

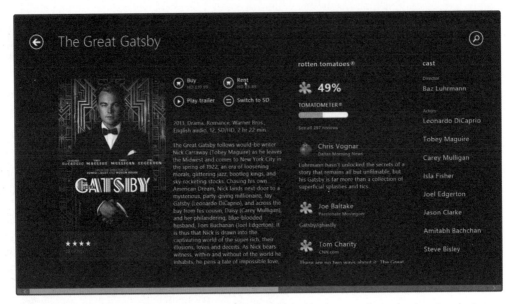

Above: With Xbox Video, you are able to search for movies and TV shows, both old and new, as well as read previous viewers' reviews.

RENTING MOVIES USING XBOX VIDEO

If you don't have a library full of videos stored on your PC, it doesn't mean you're stuck with nothing to watch. The main feature of the Xbox Video app is the huge library of films to rent and buy. There are a host of big-name movies to choose from, not to mention TV series available to watch.

1. To start watching videos, just open up the Xbox Video app and you'll be confronted with a host of titles. Tapping a tile brings up options to watch your movie, or if you're not sure, you can watch the trailer. There's also a rating from Rotten Tomatoes, the movie review website.

Hot Tip

When you rent or buy a movie, it will appear as a new tile in the Xbox Video screen, which will make it easy for you to find when you're ready to sit back and watch.

2. You can then buy the item outright or choose to rent it. If you buy a movie, you will own a copy of it and will be able watch it whenever you like, but a rental means you have a limited time period to watch it. The movie will stay on your device for 14 days after you pay for it, but once you press play, you will have just 24 hours to finish watching it.

PLAY TO DEVICES USING XBOX VIDEO

When you've got a movie on your PC, whether it's a rental from the store or one of your own files, that doesn't mean you have to watch it on your laptop or tablet while that big screen

Hot Tip

If you have your streaming devices set up using the HomeGroup feature (*see* pages 162–167), you can send video to devices, and control them, remotely.

Above: If you have enabled your other devices to stream using HomeGroup, then it's easy to watch your movie on your TV or Xbox 360.

in your living room sits idle. In the same way that Windows Media Player can enable other devices to access its content, the Xbox Video app can do the same, and with an amazing twist.

To send a video to another device, start playing it as normal on your Windows 8.1 PC. Pause it immediately and then swipe in from the right, or place your mouse in the bottom right-hand corner to show the Charms bar and choose Devices. You can take a shortcut by pressing the Windows key + K.

Hot Tip

When playing a movie to another device, you can still control it from your Windows 8.1 PC, like a high-tech remote control.

Above: Need a snack break? Use your PC as a remote control to pause the movie, and resume when you've refilled your popcorn bowl.

ENJOY PHOTOS IN WINDOWS 8.1

Aside from entertainment, Windows 8.1 is a fantastic way to enjoy your pictures and home videos too. One of the greatest things about the digital age is the ease with which we can amass huge collections of memories, from holiday snaps to those golden moments captured by the smartphones in our pockets. However, keeping on top of this digital deluge can be difficult, but Windows 8.1 can stop you getting overwhelmed, while improving your photos to enjoy in the future.

THE PICTURES LIBRARY

The default place for photos in Windows is the Pictures library, which you can access from File Explorer. It's the ideal place to store your snaps on your Windows 8.1 PC, as it's the place in which most apps and programs look for your snaps.

View Your Photos

When it comes to enjoying your snaps, you're spoiled for choice in Windows 8.1. You can choose to have your photos displayed in the Photos app or Photo Viewer on the desktop. The Photo Viewer is a rather limited desktop app that's best for quickly checking out a picture; the real

Above: The Pictures library is the go-to place for your snaps.

power is in the Photos app. In this app, photos are displayed in full screen, where you can edit your snaps, start slideshows or share them with friends. It will also import your photos straight from your camera.

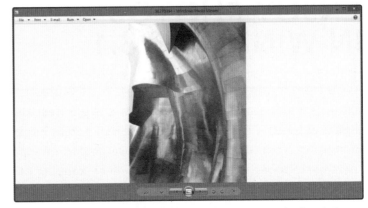

Above: The Photo Viewer app is good, but not great; use it to view snaps rather than edit them.

Organize Photos

The need for advanced organization is less important in Windows 8.1 than previous versions of Windows, where there wasn't a tool as powerful as the Photos app included.

The best way to keep snaps organized is to put them in clearly named folders in the Pictures library. The Photos app will then use these names to create an album of your memories, which you can swipe or click through.

Above: The Photos app is the one to turn to for serious viewing and editing.

Hot Tip
If you don't want to use the Pictures folder and prefer to store your photos elsewhere, you'll need to turn your new location into a library; *see page 215.*

IMPORT PHOTOS

The Photos app imports photos from your camera quickly and easily. This has historically been a difficult task, requiring you to browse to the location of your photos in Windows Explorer and then drag the files manually to your Pictures library. However, the Photo app makes it a doddle.

Connect Up Your Camera

1. Connect your camera, phone or external drive to your PC using the USB cable and open the Photos app from the Start screen.

2. Swipe in from the bottom edge to see the application commands, or if you're using a mouse and keyboard, just right-click anywhere inside the main screen, and tap or click Import. Windows 8.1 will scan your camera and show all of your snaps in a long list with a small preview.

3. Tap or click the device you want to import from

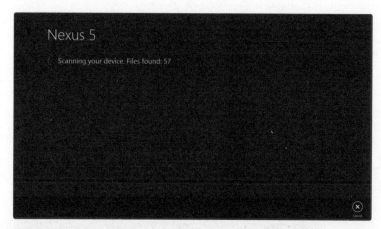

Above: Once you've connected your device, the Photos app will scan it for photo files.

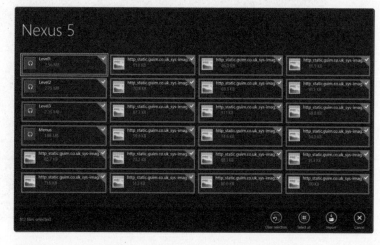

Above: Each photo that the Photos app finds will be shown as a thumbnail preview.

Hot Tip

If you import from a camera that contains images you've already copied to your PC, they will still appear in the list, but Windows 8.1 will detect them and they won't automatically be selected, so as to prevent duplication.

and then swipe or click each photo and video you want to import from the list.

4. Tap or click Import to have them copied to your Pictures library. It's important to remember that they've been copied and will remain on your camera's memory card until you delete them.

Set Settings For Importing Next Time

When you plug in your device, autoplay options will appear in the top right of the screen, asking you what you want to happen when you plug in your device next time. It will list all the available apps and actions. Just choose the one you want from the list – in this case, import using the Photos app – and it will remember those settings for the future. Next time you plug in your camera, you won't need to follow the above steps.

Above: When you add an external device, you can choose how it behaves next time you plug it in, so you can have your files organized with the minimum of fuss.

Above: Brighten up your day by choosing one of your own photos as your desktop wallpaper, or to appear on your login screen.

PERSONALIZE YOUR PC WITH PHOTOS

Once you have added photos to your PC, you can use them to give your Windows 8.1 PC a personal touch. Photos are a great way to turn Windows 8.1 into something a little more like home, making it more fun to use. You can use your photos to:

- Log into your PC
- Display as your account picture
- Use as a desktop background in Windows 8.1.

SHARING YOUR PHOTOS

Enjoying your photos is great, but it's much better to show them off to friends and family, especially the ones in your photos. That's why sharing is such an important part of Windows 8.1, and why it takes pride of place on the Charms bar.

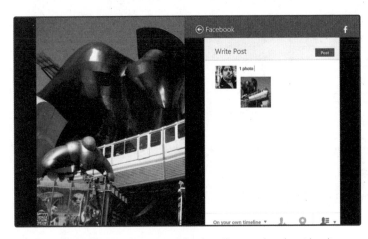

Above: Share great memories with friends via Charms, or through social media.

Above: Add location data and tag your friends when uploading from the Pictures library to Facebook in your photos.

Sharing Photos Using The Charms Bar

You can send pictures to friends at any time using charms, and it's much quicker than using individual services like Facebook and Twitter, simply because they all appear automatically with the Share charm.

1. To start sharing, open the Photos app (or any other app you're using to view and edit your photos). In the app, go to the folder containing the photos you want to share, or a single photo if you want. Access the Charms bar and then choose Share. The app you're using to share, be it Facebook, Twitter or whatever you use, will be listed.

Hot Tip

Before you can start sharing with your favourite social media service, you need to download it as an app from the Windows Store and make sure you're logged in. Once that's done, you'll find it in the Share charm list.

2. Choose the app you want to use from the list, and it will open inside the Photos app, taking up the right-hand side of the screen. Use the service as normal.

How To Print From Windows Store Apps

If you have a photo printer, you can reproduce high-quality snaps to share with friends and family the old-fashioned way. Modern photo printers can rival the professionals for quality, and you'll save money too, even if you're using top-quality photo paper and ink. You can see a guide to setting up your printer in our Getting Started chapter on pages 83–84.

Hot Tip

The options you see in the More settings section come from the printer manufacturer, so your choices will vary depending on the printer. You can tweak settings such as quality and the number of copies. When everything is set up, tap or click Print.

1. Find a photo you want to print, then tap or click it to open it.

2. Go to the Charms bar and then tap Devices (or hit the Windows key + K) and choose a printer from the list. You'll see a preview of what you're printing, along with the number of copies and the page orientation on the preview pane.

Above: You can print photos straight from the Pictures app using the Devices charm.

UPLOAD PHOTOS TO ONEDRIVE

The OneDrive service, which provides Windows 8.1's cloud storage, is a great way to back up your photos to make sure that a tech disaster can't destroy your precious photos and memories. You get a whopping 7 GB of storage absolutely free with Windows 8.1, which is plenty for most people's libraries, and with the easy uploading features, there's no reason not to back your photos up to the cloud.

Above: Save your photos in OneDrive's cloud and they will be secure.

Make OneDrive A Pictures Library

Because your OneDrive folders are baked into Windows 8.1 like any other hard drive, you can store your photos online, and use them as with any other library. Find the folder within OneDrive, right-click and choose Include in library, followed by the Pictures option. It will now behave exactly as the traditional method, but instead of being on your PC's hard drive, it's safely stored in the cloud.

TAKING PHOTOS WITH YOUR WINDOWS 8.1 PC

The beauty of Windows 8.1 devices is that most come with cameras built in. Laptop users will have one built into the top of the screen, which is designed for video-calling apps such as Skype, but those using Windows 8.1 tablets will have a secondary snapper on the back, which is great for taking photos.

To take photos on your Windows 8.1 device, you need to use the Camera app on your Start screen. When the app starts for the first time, it will ask permission to use the camera hardware on your PC, so just click or tap Allow.

How To Take A Photo

If your device has a rear camera, the app will default to this, and you can take a photo by tapping anywhere on the screen. Once it's taken, you can swipe right on a touch screen device to access the camera roll, or right-click anywhere if using a mouse and keyboard, and click the camera roll button.

Hot Tip

Want to take a great selfie? Windows 8.1 has a timer for taking pictures remotely. Right-click to bring up the Options menu and tap the Timer option. Tap once for three seconds, twice for ten seconds and a third time to cancel the timer.

Above: Windows tablets are particularly good for taking photos, as they have a built-in camera; just tap the Camera app tile to get started.

Options When Taking A Photo Or Video

You can make a host of changes to your camera settings, which can help you take better photos whatever the conditions. Whether it's shooting in the dark, low light conditions or just trying to make the family shot look its best, it's well worth tweaking the settings before you start.

Above: Improve your photos by taking advantage of the camera settings options.

By right-clicking or swiping up from the bottom, you can:

- Set a self-timer for group shots
- Change the exposure for better lighting, especially in dim conditions
- Toggle the flash on/off/automatic for illuminating subjects in the dark

However, there are a host of additional options, which can really help you get more from your shots.

ACCESS THE ADVANCED OPTIONS

To access the advanced photo settings options, go to the Settings charm by swiping from the right, or placing your mouse into the bottom-right corner of the screen and hit Options.

Changing The Photo Aspect Ratio

A new settings pane will appear on the right of the screen. From here, you can change the aspect ratio of your shots, which means the shape of your photo. A 4:3 photo is nearly square, while 16:9 is the same aspect as your monitor. On the other hand, 16:10 is narrower, but you can fit more into your shot.

> ## Hot Tip
> If your Windows 8.1 PC has two cameras, which is common on hybrids and tablets, you can switch to view either one by clicking the icon on the camera settings menu. Just swipe up from the bottom or right-click and press Change camera.

Showing Or Hiding Grid Lines

You can add grid lines to the camera app, which can help you line up your shots for improved composition. The grid lines will enable you to level with the horizon, and keep your pictures in proportion for dramatically improved snaps.

Turning Location Info On Or Off

Windows 8.1 lets you add location data to your photos, which can be used by third-party apps to organize your libraries. Location reporting is on as default in Windows 8.1, but you can turn location reporting off or on in the Options menu.

Above: Enable grid lines in the Camera app, and your photos will be better composed.

Hot Tip

On some Windows 8.1 tablets, the Camera app automatically takes several photos in a row (known as a photo loop) when you take a photo. If your device supports this, every time you take a photo, you'll see a rectangle appear in the bottom corner. You can then check out all the options and save your favourite one, which is a great way to get the perfect people shot.

TROUBLESHOOTING & MAINTENANCE

KEEP WINDOWS 8.1 RUNNING SMOOTHLY

Like any machine, your Windows PC needs regular maintenance. Luckily, the system is full of fantastic tools to keep things running smoothly, and the best news is that most can be automated so that you don't even have to think about it.

OPTIMIZE YOUR DRIVES

Performance can suffer over time, and you may experience a gradual reduction in performance unless you keep your PC well maintained. The main offender is your hard drive. Like anything, the more clutter and mess, the less well it runs, and there's also fragmentation.

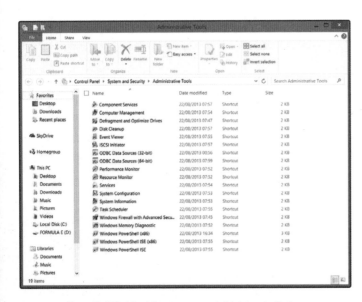

Above: You'll find the defragging program in Administrative Tools.

Disk Defragmenting

Your PC's hard drive is like a library and, when the library is empty, it's easy to keep all the John Grisham books together. However, over time, when the library gets full, there may not be room to keep them all together, so they get spread across different shelves. When you want to loan out all the Grisham books, it will take you longer to find them. The same is true for your hard drive. Disk defragmenting tidies up all your data, and puts it back together.

Use The Optimize Drives Feature

Windows 8.1 has a built-in tool for defragging your drive. By default, it's set to run every week, but you can do it manually by following these steps:

1. Open Optimize Drives by searching 'admin' on the Start screen, and then tapping or clicking Administrative Tools. In that menu, choose Defragment and Optimize Drives. Under Status, tap or click the drive you want to optimize. To help you determine if the drive needs to be optimized, tap or click Analyze.

2. After Windows has finished analysing the drive, check the Current status column to see whether you need to optimize the drive. If the drive is more than 10 per cent fragmented, you should optimize the drive now. Tap or click Optimize to start the process.

Hot Tip
If you can't click the Analyze option because it's greyed out, it means your disk should already be fully defragged, so there's no need to worry.

Hot Tip
You can have your drives optimized automatically to make sure they are always in top condition. To do this, open the Optimize Drives window and check that scheduled optimization reads 'on'.

Right: Click Analyze to assess whether the selected drive needs to be optimized.

DISK CLEANUP

The Disk Cleanup feature has been buried in Windows 8.1, but it's a great tool for quickly de-cluttering your operating system, which has the dual benefit of making your PC run more quickly and simultaneously saving precious hard drive space.

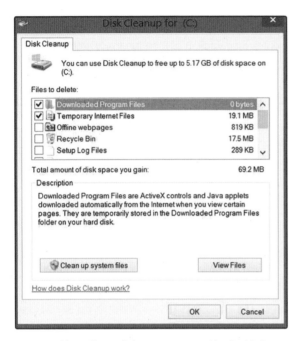

Above: Choose which items you want to delete for disk cleanup.

Using Disk Cleanup To Delete System Files

1. To open Disk Cleanup from the desktop, search Administrative Tools and then double-tap or double-click Disk Cleanup from the next list. In the Drives list, tap or click the drive that you want to clean up, then tap or click OK.

2. You'll now see a host of checkboxes for the types of clutter that can be deleted. Tick as many as you want to delete. A running total of the amount of space you can save will be displayed underneath the list. Press OK when you're done to have those files deleted.

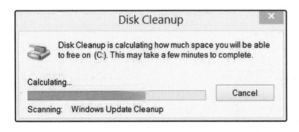

Above: As you tick which items you want to delete, a running total will tell you how much disk space will be freed.

Hot Tip

System files that eat up disk space can range from Windows Update log files, which aren't essential and can make a dent in your disk space, to User file history, which is very useful but takes up a lot of room.

3. If you really want to start saving space, you can opt to clean up system files. This will include a host of Windows background information which, while not unnecessary clutter, is not essential for Windows 8.1's day-to-day running.

MORE CLEANUP OPTIONS

If you want to free up even more space on your PC, tap or click Clean up system files and wait for your system to be scanned. A tab called More Options will appear at the top of this window. There are two options for saving hard-drive space on your PC:

Programs And Features

This feature brings up a new window that lists all your installed apps. You can uninstall – which means safely delete – any programs you no longer use. The Size column shows how much space each program uses.

System Restore And Shadow Copies

Delete all but the most recent restore point on the drive. You can often have scores of updates saved in reserve, but as long as your PC is working well, you can safely delete them. This option will remove all but the last restore point, so it won't put you at risk.

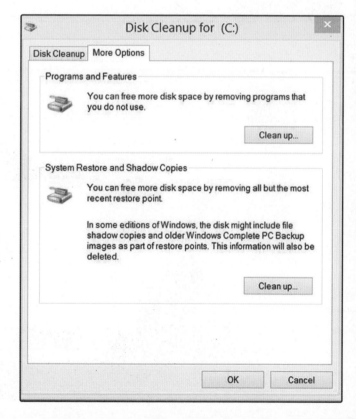

Right: You can save even more space by deleting unused programs and unnecessary backups.

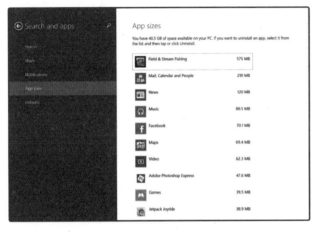

Above: You can easily see how much disk space is used by your apps.

KEEP ON TOP OF WINDOWS APPS

Windows 8.1 Start screen apps won't appear in the desktop cleanup options, but you can still get a summary of how much room they're taking up. Search for 'uninstall apps' on the Start screen, and choose Uninstall apps to free up disk space. You'll then see a list of all the apps on your system and how much space they're using. Tap any app and hit Uninstall to delete it from your PC.

OTHER MAINTENANCE TASKS

Aside from de-cluttering your PC's files, there are plenty of other maintenance tasks that are too often forgotten and harder to automate. Make sure you keep this list handy to make sure your PC stays in tiptop condition.

Clean Screen

Keeping your screen clean is essential and will ensure your display is easy to see, but it's important to use proper solution and a lint-free cloth.

Clean Keyboard

Studies have found the humble keyboard can harbour more germs than a toilet seat, so keeping it clean is imperative. What's more, buttons can start to seize with dirt and grime,

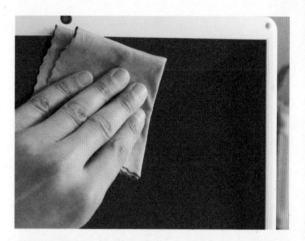

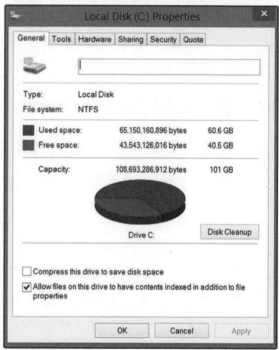

Above: Check regularly how much free space you have left.

Hot Tip

Keep an eye on your hard drive's capacity to avoid a nasty shock when running out of room. To check free space, open up File Explorer, right-click the C: drive and choose Properties.

which is especially problematic on laptops. Use antibacterial wipes to keep the keys germ free and invest in a compressed-air canister to blow dirt free from the crevices.

Create A System Image Backup

When you have your PC the way you want it, you can take an exact snapshot of your computer's system so that it can be restored if you have a problem with your computer. You can set this system image by searching 'file history' on the Start screen (the File History control panel, not the main File History interface) and choose System Image Backup in the bottom left. See page 213 for a full explanation of how to set up and restore this kind of backup.

SPEED UP YOUR PC WITH POWER PLANS

Like a racing car, Windows 8.1 can manage its power, so that you can put the emphasis on performance or efficiency. This is especially important for laptop users, who want top performance when plugged into the power, but longer battery when out on the move.

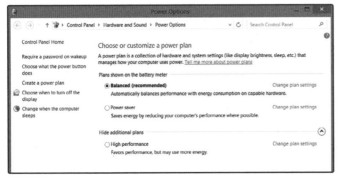

Above: Balanced is the best all-round power plan to use.

What Are Power Plans?

Windows 8.1's power plans are profiles that tell the system how intensively to work. If your system is using the highest power it will run at its fastest rate, but this will have a negative effect on battery life. When set to an economical power plan, the system runs less quickly but the battery will last longer.

What Power Plans Are Available?

- **Balanced**: Offers full performance when you need it and saves power when you don't. This is the best power plan for most people.

- **Power saver:** Saves power by reducing PC performance and screen brightness. If you're using a laptop, this plan can help you get the most from a single battery charge.

- **High performance:** Maximizes screen brightness and might increase PC performance. This plan uses a lot more energy, so your laptop battery won't last as long between charges.

Changing Power Plans

If you're using a laptop, it's really simple to switch plans. Just click the battery icon in the notification area at the far right of the taskbar. You will see two plans – Balanced or Power saver. Use the Power saver option when away from the mains, and Balanced when connected. If your PC has InstantGo power management built in, there may only be one plan listed, but it can be fully customized.

If you aren't using a laptop, search for 'power options' on the Start screen and choose it from the list. Select the power plan you'd like to use, or tap or click Show additional plans.

> 1 hr 29 min (45%) remaining
>
> Battery #1: 45% remaining
> Battery #2: Not present
>
> Select a power plan:
> ◉ Balanced
> ○ Power saver
>
> ⓘ Your current brightness setting might reduce battery life.
>
> Adjust screen brightness
> More power options

Above: Laptops offer a quick way to change between power plans.

Create A Custom Power Plan

You can create your own custom power plan in Windows 8.1, where you can enable or disable options to have your PC work your way.

To create your own custom plan, open the Power Options menu and tap or click Create a power plan. You can base your plan on an existing one, so if you want your custom setting to be heavy on power, choose High

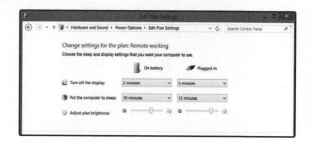

Above: You can customize the settings for a power plan.

performance. Name your setting and press Next. You can then choose a combination of display timing, sleep settings and screen brightness for battery and mains power. Press Create to finish.

FIX WINDOWS PROBLEMS

While Windows 8.1 is the most advanced version of Microsoft's operating system, things can still go wrong from time to time. However, the beauty of the new Windows is that there are even more ways to fix problems and with this chapter to help, you'll have everything you need.

RESET YOUR PC

When things went wrong in previous versions of Windows, or your PC got slowed down over time, a reinstallation of the operating system was the only option.

Above: Resetting your PC is the only way back to a genuinely clean, shop-fresh system, which hopefully runs faster. As the function is now built into the system, it's much easier than reinstalling from a disk.

Why Do You Need To Refresh Your PC?

Over time, the back end of Windows can get messy. The huge numbers of files, downloaded programs and other waste can be cleaned up easily, but other issues can come into play.

One of the biggest problems is the 'registry', which holds all the information Windows needs to run. Over time, changes to the system mean that the registry gets full of rubbish, which slows down your system. While there are registry cleaner tools on the Internet that can help – CCleaner is especially good – if your system is that slow, reinstalling is the only way back to a genuinely 'shop-fresh' system.

No More Reinstalls

Reinstalling used to be the bane of any Windows user's existence and in previous versions of the operating system, it was an all-too-frequent occurrence. It meant digging out your recovery disc, backing everything up – a long and complex process – and then the hassle of setting everything up again.

In Windows 8.1, the ability to reset your PC has been built in, so if you find your PC crawling to a halt, you can press a button and have everything reset, without the difficult set-up. What's more, there's even an option to reset all the system files but keep your own files and settings intact. Here's how:

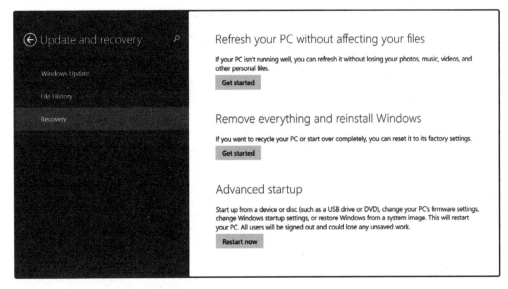

Above: When resetting your PC, the option with least impact is Refresh your PC without affecting files.

Perform A Partial Reset

You can solve PC problems such as slow performance in Windows 8.1 by heading to the PC Settings menu, accessible via the Charms bar. You can access that by swiping in from the right, or placing your mouse in the bottom right-hand corner of the screen. In the next list, choose Update and recovery and, when the left-hand pane changes, choose Recovery.

Hot Tip

You should use the Refresh your PC without affecting your files option where possible. Completely resetting your PC will mean the loss of all your precious files and photos, while refreshing will hopefully clear your problem, and return your system with everything as normal.

Complete A Full Reset

If a partial reset doesn't do the trick, a full reset might be in order. This should be a final resort, after you've tried working through the various resolutions to problems in this chapter.

The full reset will delete every file and setting on your PC, and return it to the same state as the day you bought it. Just press Get started, but make sure everything is backed up on to removable storage, as all drives will be wiped.

USE SYSTEM RESTORE

If your problems have been caused by a specific event, such as a bad installation or a failed update, it's extremely easy to roll back time and revert your Windows 8.1 PC to the way it was before. The System Restore feature automatically creates an image of your system when a critical event happens.

What Is A System Restore?

System Restore is a feature in Windows 8.1 that enables you to turn back time on your system, and have a top-running system resurrected on your PC. In the background, Windows 8.1 takes snapshots of your system in case things go wrong.

Revert To A Restore Point

You can revert to a restore point by again heading to the Recovery menu in the Settings charm. Under Advanced Startup,

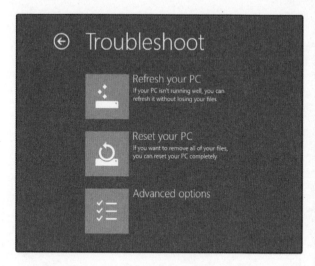

Above: Use the Advanced options under Advanced Startup to get to a list of restore points that your PC can be reverted to.

Above: Use System Restore to revert to the latest available system image, or select a specific one.

Hot Tip

If you're not sure which System Restore point to pick, just pick the last date on which you're sure your system was working properly.

Above: When creating a system image, you can choose whether to save it on a hard drive, DVD or in a network location.

tap or click Restart Now. Windows will start to reboot and you will enter a new menu deep inside the underbelly of the operating system. Choose Troubleshoot and then Reset your PC, followed by Advanced options. The System Restore button will be on the following menu and you'll be asked to enter your password.

Follow the steps until you reach a list of points to which it can be restored. Each will have a description and a date, which should help you pinpoint the system change that prompted the restore point to be created. If you know the event that caused your issues, then choose the one before. Press Next, and your system will be restored and your PC will restart. When you're returned to Windows 8.1, your system should be working.

RESTORE FROM YOUR OWN SYSTEM IMAGE

If you're runnning Windows 8 you can create your own restore point, rather than rely on Windows 8.1's. This restore point means capturing a complete copy of your system, with every file, wallpaper and setting. It's a good idea to do this at a point at which you're completely happy with your system and its set up.

Create Your Own Restore Point

You can set your restore point by searching 'file history' on the Start screen and clicking the option in the results. In the bottom left corner is an option to create a System Image Backup. In the next window, choose where you'd like to save your system, press Next and then Start Backup.

Restore Your System Image

To restore your own system image, head back to the Recovery menu, go to Advanced Startup and hit the Troubleshoot option again. Choose Advanced options, followed by System Image Recovery, making sure that the device to which you backed up your PC is connected. When the recovery tool loads, choose the account you're going to recover, enter your password and the tool will find your settings.

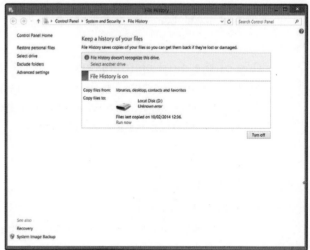

Above: Go to File History to create a System Image Backup.

Hot Tip
You can restore to a USB hard drive, CD/DVD or somewhere on your network. However, as it's a copy of your entire system, you'll need plenty of hard-disk space.

SOLVE STARTUP ISSUES

One of the most alarming events in Windows is when your PC fails to start, and for Windows novices, it can be a serious issue. A PC that fails to start gives the user very little to work with, but follow these steps and you can overcome startup issues in no time.

WINDOWS 8.1 WON'T START

If your PC won't boot up at all, the troubleshooting tools can help you to roll back your PC to the last good configuration, or access Windows 8.1 in safe mode. (Troubleshooting will start automatically if Windows fails to start; you can also insert the recovery media that came with your PC). Safe mode is a basic state Windows can log into, which strips out everything bar the bare essentials. It's useful when something in Windows is causing a conflict or has broken, and you can log in without that rogue program running.

Above: Safe Mode is a way of accessing Windows in a limited fashion, in order to diagnose the problem that is causing Windows to malfunction.

Log In Using Safe Mode

Unlike older versions of Windows, you can't press F8 at boot to bring up a boot menu to log into safe mode.

If Windows has detected a problem that's caused a boot failure, it should load up the diagnostic tools automatically. You can then choose Troubleshoot and then Safe Mode to log into your account.

Force Your PC Into Safe Mode

If Windows isn't loading the diagnostic tools, then all is not

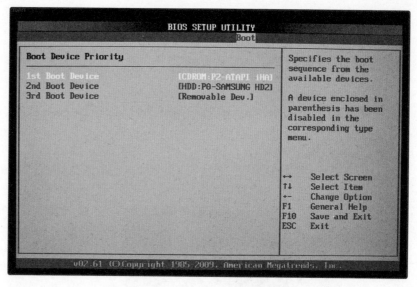

Above: BIOS enables you to change the order of the drives in which the PC looks for recovery media.

lost. Your PC should ship with recovery media, which can be used to load the Windows system in the event of a complete failure. Head to your manufacturer's supplied contents and find this media, which is often on a CD or USB key. Insert this and restart your computer. This should give you the option to access the troubleshooting tools.

Change Boot Priority

Your computer should look for recovery media by default. Every Windows PC has an order in which it looks for Windows files, and the CD drive or USB will normally be searched before the hard drive. However, if your PC has been set to look for Windows files on the hard drive first, and that is broken, your recovery media will have no effect. Fear not, as you can change this:

1. As soon as you start your computer, press F1 before Windows loads to open up the BIOS. This is the built-in program that's stored on your PC's processor. Its job is to get all the components of your PC communicating in order to load up the operating system.

2. In the BIOS menus, choose the Boot tab and then look at the Boot priority menu. The top location is the first place your PC will look, and you can move the order about by using the F5 and F6 keys.

3. Move the CD drive or USB to the top and then save the changes. When you restart, your PC will now find your Windows boot media, and load the troubleshooting tools.

WINDOWS' STARTUP TOOLS EXPLAINED

Startup Repair Tool

Once you've got Windows 8.1's troubleshooting menu to load, there are a variety of tools that can solve a PC that's not booting, or not starting correctly.

1. To access them, tap or click the Advanced options and choose Startup repair.

2. Tap or click the option in the troubleshooting list, and Windows 8.1 will go into a diagnostic mode.

3. Select the Windows account that's not booting and you'll be asked for your login information. Windows will then look for issues with your PC and attempt to fix any problems to get you into Windows.

STARTUP SETTINGS

Windows 8.1 enables you to change a host of settings that can lead to common startup faults.

1. Choose Startup Settings from the list and at the next menu, tap or click Restart.

2. A list of numbered options will appear, and you just need to choose the correct one, pressing the corresponding number on your computer's keyboard.

Startup Settings

Press a number to choose from the options below:

Use number keys or functions keys F1-F9.

1) Enable debugging
2) Enable boot logging
3) Enable low-resolution video
4) Enable Safe Mode
5) Enable Safe Mode with Networking
6) Enable Safe Mode with Command Prompt
7) Disable driver signature enforcement
8) Disable early launch anti-malware protection
9) Disable automatic restart after failure

Press F10 for more options
Press Enter to return to your operating system

Above: Startup Settings lists troubleshooting modes.

Enable Debugging Mode

An advanced troubleshooting in which where information is transmitted to another computer or device that's running a debugger. For professionals only.

Enable Boot Logging

This setting loads up Windows and keeps a text log of everything that happens. It's stored as ntbtlog.txt in the C:/Windows folder. If Windows, starts you can open it to see the cause of problems, and if not, you can use safe mode to go and take a look. If neither option works, boot to the Command Line and type: d:\windows\ntbtlog.txt.

Enable Low-Resolution Video

This starts Windows with the most basic graphic settings. This can eliminate screen incompatibility and if your graphics card has failed, you may still be able to log in.

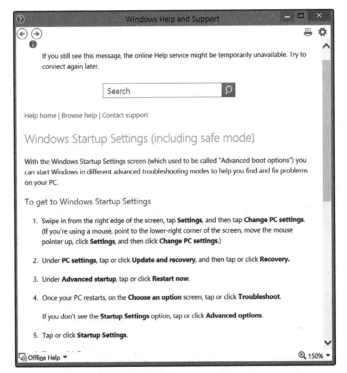

Above: Access Safe Mode from Advanced Startup Options in the Startup Settings menu.

Enable Safe Mode

This is a state of Windows in which only the minimum settings, drivers and system files are loaded. This minimizes the chance of a hardware or software conflict or failure, and enables you to make critical changes to the system that can resolve problems, or at least allow you to back up your files before more drastic action.

Enable Safe Mode With Networking

As above, but in the standard safe mode, even Internet access is blocked. Safe mode with networking enables you to access the web, which enables you to run critical updates or fetch drivers from the web.

Enable Safe Mode With Command Prompt

This loads up the Command Prompt, which is a basic screen into which you can type written commands. If Windows refuses to boot under any of the other safe-mode options, choose this to access the boot log outlined in the boot logging section on the opposite page.

Disable Driver Signature Enforcement

This enables non-approved drivers to be installed in Windows. This is not recommended for fixing Windows problems.

Disable Early Launch Anti-malware Protection

This boots Windows and launches an anti-malware program to sweep for viruses, spyware and other potential issues. Best used if you suspect a virus has caused Windows startup problems.

Disable Automatic Restart After Failure

If your PC is in a loop of failed restarts and reboots, then use this option to break the cycle.

Above: Starting up in Safe Mode can help eliminate the default settings and basic device drivers as possible causes of problems.

FIX A SLOW PC

If you find your PC is slowing down, don't reach for the reset button quite yet. Aside from the basic maintenance tasks we mentioned earlier, there are a few more ways to speed up a slouching system. Here, we run through all the options.

BASIC MAINTENANCE

If your PC is running slowly, check off these options first before taking further action.

Disk Cleanup

Unnecessary files can slow down your PC, so use Windows 8.1's built-in Disk Cleanup tool to get rid of computer clutter. You can access the tool by searching for 'administrative tools' on the Start screen. Turn to pages 220–221 for a full guide to using the Disk Cleanup feature.

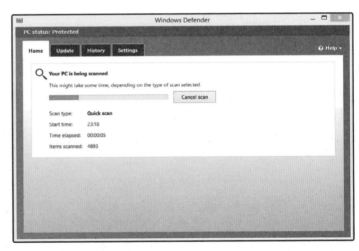

Above: Use Windows Defender to run a full scan to check for virus or spyware infections.

Check For Malware And Viruses

A slow PC can be caused by malware and if your PC has suddenly slowed down, it could be due to a virus or spyware infection. Windows Defender is our friend, here. Search for it on the Start screen and run a full scan.

Check Memory Usage

If your PC is performing badly, press Ctrl + Alt + Delete and choose Task Manager from the list. Tap or click More details at the bottom, and you'll see a full list of running processes. Check out the levels of CPU, Memory and Disk it's using. If non-essential programs are eating up your resources, you can tap or click them and choose End task.

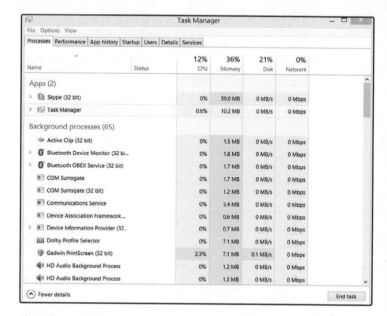

Above: Open up Task Manager to check how much memory programs are using.

Delete Programs

If installed programs are eating away at your system memory and CPU, then removing them altogether might be the best option. Search 'programs' on the Start screen and choose 'Programs and features' from the list. You will see a list of your programs and their impact on your hard drive. Choose any program you want to remove and click Uninstall to banish it for ever.

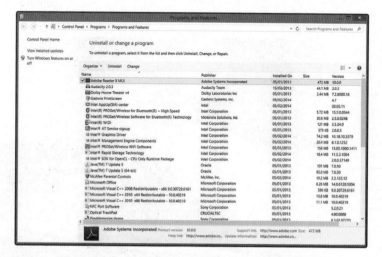

Above: In Programs and features, you can choose to delete items to free space.

TURN OFF ANIMATIONS

If your PC is really struggling with speed problems, it may be wise to take more drastic action. Windows 8.1 is filled with small animations, which give it its slick and polished feel. However, this can take its toll. Luckily, you can switch off these effects to save graphics and processor power. Here's how you turn off effects:

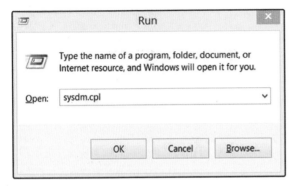

Above: Open Run and type in sysdm.cpl to get to System Properties in order to turn off animations.

1. Press Windows key + R to open the Run box, and type sysdm.cpl before hitting Enter. The System Properties window will open.

2. Go to the Advanced tab and click on Settings in the Performance section.

3. This will open a new window. Choose Adjust for best performance and press OK. Windows will look considerably less polished when you return, but it should run a lot more quickly.

SPEED UP YOUR START

Windows 8.1's boot times are a dramatic improvement on previous versions of the operating system, but after a while, it can take a long time for your PC to become responsive when loading up. There are multiple reasons for this, but the key complaint is installed applications that default to starting as soon as your PC does. The combined stress of loading 10 programs at once can mean it's an agonizing wait for Windows to become usable.

Disable Apps From Starting With Windows

The Task Manager in Windows 8.1 has been upgraded to come to the rescue of sluggish starters. If you are not sure which apps to kill, try a free third-party app like SysInternals' free Autoruns (http://autoruns.en.softonic.com) which will do the work for you.

1. Press Ctrl + Alt + Delete and choose Task Manager.

2. Choose the Startup tab from the top and a list of all the programs and services set to start with Windows will appear, and their impact on the time your PC takes to start will be shown as 'low', 'medium' or 'high'.

3. Many of these items will be non-essential, so just click or tap them before hitting Disable. Remember, programs can be pinned to the taskbar or Start screen, so they can be launched easily without affecting your boot time.

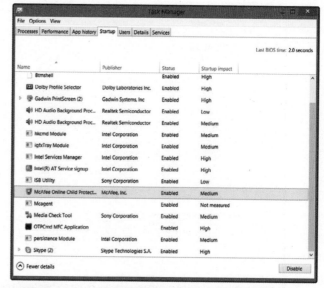

Above: If you don't need an application to open on startup, you can disable it in the Startup pane of Task Manager and it may speed up boot time.

FIX A PC THAT CRASHES

If your PC is crashing, or programs regularly stop responding, there can be many causes, and finding the root of the problem is key. Luckily, Windows 8.1 is full of tools that can help you get to the bottom of crashes.

DEAL WITH CRASHES

If a program crashes or becomes unresponsive, you need to bring up the Task Manager by pressing Ctrl + Alt + Delete. Choose Task Manager and the program that's failed from the list. If it has crashed, it should say 'not responding' next to it. Choose it from the list and tap or click End task to close it.

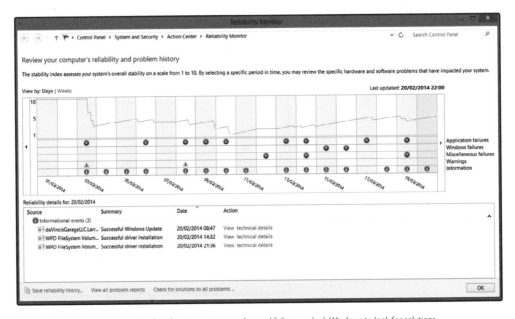

Above: Use Reliability Monitor to check and assess program crashes and failures and ask Windows to look for solutions.

Check Reliability Monitor

You can check the Reliability Monitor in Windows 8.1 to check for programs or services that have crashed or failed, and the app will show you the occurrence of reliability issues. It's a top diagnostic tool, and while most of it is too advanced to be of use to most users, it can help you fix problems with your PC.

Search for 'reliability' on the Start screen and you'll see a history of all program issues on a graph, with full details beneath. Your PC will be prone to more crashes that you might realize, and you can view details of each one. However, tap or click Check for solutions to all problems, and Windows will look for fixes to those problems.

Check Windows 8.1 Event Viewer

If your PC is suffering from regular crashes, checking the built-in Event Viewer can reveal more information about what's causing errors. Events are classified either as an error, a warning or

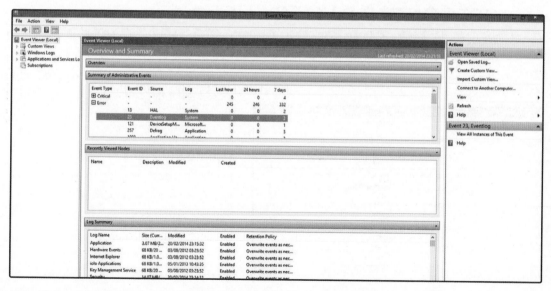

Above: The Event Viewer allows you to view event logs on significant system events, to help pinpoint causes of problems.

information. An error is a significant problem, such as loss of data; a warning is an event that might indicate a possible future problem; an information event describes the successful operation of a program, driver or service.

Much of the information in the Event Viewer can be helpful if you're having a problem with your computer but you're not sure of the cause. If your computer suffers from the dreaded Blue Screen of Death, the Event Viewer may provide more information about the cause. For example, an error event in the System log section may inform of you which driver crashed, which in turn can help you pin down a buggy driver or a faulty hardware component.

Just look for the error message associated with the time your computer froze or restarted. The error codes listed in the Event Viewer can be searched online, and it might mean the difference between fixing your PC at home and seeking expensive professional help.

GET LONGER BATTERY LIFE

Windows 8.1 devices don't enjoy the kind of battery life that most traditional tablets and smartphones do, because of the types of components used inside. The hugely increased power of a Windows 8.1 laptop or tablet means that all-day usage isn't easily achieved. However, with a few insider tips and tricks, you should be able to extend your usage.

Above: Edit power saving settings with a custom Power Plan.

Use Power Plans

Firstly, choose a low-usage power plan when working away from the mains. You can switch to this by tapping or clicking the battery icon on the taskbar. You can also create your own custom battery-saving Power Plan by following our guide on page 225.

Reduce Display Brightness

One of the biggest battery-draining offenders is your PC's display, kicking out as it does pin-sharp HD visuals. Using your keyboard's function keys to turn down the brightness can help. Alternatively, tap or click the Screen option in the Settings charm (before tapping PC Settings).

Some PCs adjust screen brightness automatically, based on how much light there is in the room. You'll need to turn this off before you can adjust the brightness.

Above: Reduce display brightness to save battery power – do this via your keyboard, monitor buttons or the Settings charm.

Disconnect

Turning off or unplugging devices that you aren't using will help to save battery. USB devices use your PC's power just by being connected, so unplug memory sticks, mice or other peripherals when you're not using them. Also, take out CDs from your drives. If you don't have wireless, turn off the adapter altogether in the Settings charm. This will avoid your PC looking for available networks and wasting power.

FIX DEVICES THAT AREN'T WORKING

If you suffer from a hardware problem, it normally means hours on the phone to tech support, a trip back to the shop, or worse, a journey to the dump. However, you can fix many problems with tools in Windows.

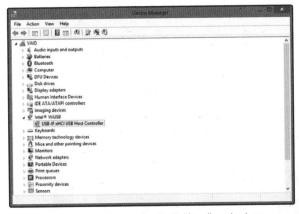

Above: Device Manager (*see* Hot Tip) lists all your hardware.

FIX PRINT PROBLEMS

Check The Power

Make sure that the printer's electrical cord is plugged into the mains and that the power switch is turned on. If you're printing to a shared printer or a printer on a network, make sure that all necessary computers and routers are switched on too.

Check The Connection

Make sure that the printer cable is properly connected from the printer to your PC, which is usually a USB cable. If you're printing wirelessly, make sure that the printer's wireless option is switched on and available. There may also be wireless tests with your printer's software, so check the manual.

Above: Make sure you check the physical connections to your printer first – i.e. that power and USB cables are properly plugged in.

Install Drivers

Printers rely on drivers to work, which are small pieces of software that act as the go-between for your Windows PC and the printer. If you don't have the right driver, your printer won't work. While this should be done automatically, here's how to find new drivers for your printer.

1. Windows Update might have an updated version of your printer driver. Go to the Settings charm, choose Update and recovery and then Windows Update. Check for updates with your printer connected, and restart your PC afterwards.

2. Install software from the printer manufacturer. If your printer came with a disc, this is the best place to look.

3. Download and install the updated driver yourself. You can search for the correct driver software on the manufacturer's website.

Right: Find up-to-date drivers to download on your printer manufacturer's website.

Hot Tip

You can see every device on your system in the Device Manager option. Just search for 'hardware' on the Start screen, choose the System option and click or tap the Device Manager option in the top left. Here, you can locate any piece of hardware, whether it's inside your PC or a peripheral like a printer or scanner. If there's a problem, a yellow warning sign will show.

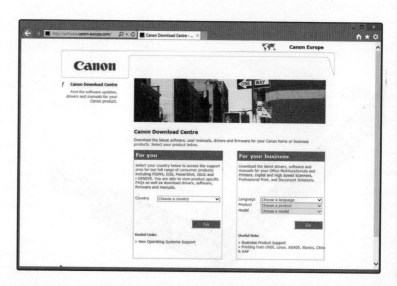

UPGRADING PC HARDWARE

Some types of Windows PC enable you to upgrade your hardware, which can vastly improve your experience. Whether it's installing a new hard drive or more memory, you don't have to buy a whole new system to get better performance.

OPENING UP YOUR PC

Changing hardware is not for the faint-hearted, but the good news is that it's generally a simple job. Desktop PCs have the most options for adding hardware, but you can also change hard drives and RAM on laptops. Tablets, hybrids and Ultrabooks allow for little in the way of hardware upgrades. Before you upgrade your PC, it's important to remember that this kind of activity will void your warranty, and to use an anti-static wristband or ground yourself by touching the PC case before handling RAM.

Installing A New Hard Drive

Desktop PCs use 3.5-in (8.8 cm) drives, while laptops will use a smaller 2.5-in (6.3 cm) drive. The former will usually allow for multiple drives, and it's just a case of slotting it into a free space and connecting a SATA cable to your PC's motherboard. Laptops are less simple, as only one drive is supported, but you can buy a kit to help you transfer your data.

Left: It is relatively straightforward to install a new hard disk drive into your desktop PC.

Changing To SSD

An SSD drive is a hard drive which uses electronic 'flash' storage rather than a spinning disc. They're much more expensive with less volume, but are much faster and far less likely to corrupt or crash. Moving Windows files to an SSD is the single biggest performance improvement you can make to your PC.

Upgrading Optical Drive

Whilst not an easy job on a laptop, desktop PCs can handle multiple CD drives and usually have spare slots for their installation. You can upgrade to Blu-ray for watching HD movies and burning huge data discs.

Above: A solid-state drive (SSD) offers better performance and reliability than a hard disk drive (HDD).

Adding More RAM

A simple and cheap upgrade to your PC, the only problem is buying the right type. You can use the tool at www.crucial.com to find out the type you need for your PC or laptop. Upgrading your RAM can improve a sluggish PC which has problems when running lots of apps simultaneously.

Replacing Laptop Battery

Most laptops will have a removable battery, which can be removed by unclipping the catches underneath your machine or by simply sliding it out. However, every battery is different, and you will need to buy the exact type for your laptop model.

Above: Make sure you buy the exact battery needed for your laptop make and model.

SOLVE SOUND PROBLEMS

Check Your Sound Card

Enter 'device manager' on the Start screen search box, then tap or click Device Manager. Double-tap or double-click Sound, video and game controllers to expand that category. If a sound card is listed, you have one installed. If there's an orange exclamation mark here, there is a problem with the device.

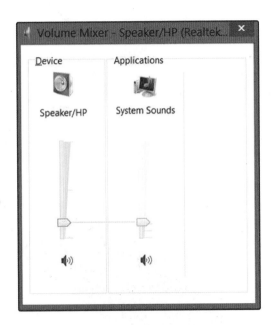

Above: If you can't hear sound, check that all volume controls are turned up and mute buttons are off.

Check Volumes

A common mistake is to have your volume turned down, and because there are so many volume controls in Windows 8.1, it can be easy to miss one. To check, enter 'adjust system volume' in the search box on the Start screen and tap or click Adjust system volume. Move the slider up to increase the volume and make sure the mute button isn't turned on. If this doesn't work, check the volume for the program you're trying to hear sound in. For example, Windows Media Player has its own.

Check Windows Update

Try running an update by going to the Settings charm and then Update and recovery, followed by Windows Update. This will look for drivers for your sound card, which may fix the problem.

MORE WAYS TO GET HELP

No simple guide to Windows can cover every eventuality and problem, but if you can't fix a problem from these pages, there are plenty of ways to get help.

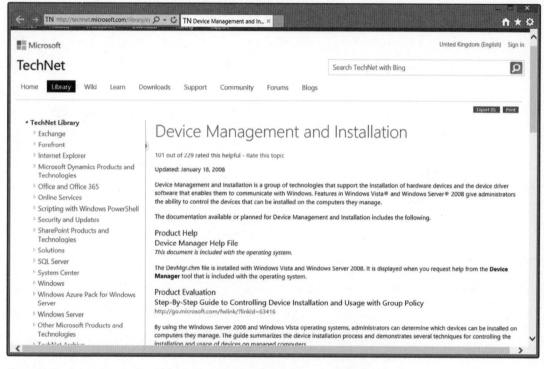

Above: Windows help topics are accessed online; just go to Settings and select Help, and you will be taken there.

Hot Tip

The Internet is full of forums that can help you with more obscure problems. Good support forums include www.eightforums.com and www.tomshardware.co.uk/forum/. Googling the problem is often the best way to find a solution.

Help Files

Windows has a huge number of help files within it, and any aspect of the operating system you're not sure about will be found here. Unlike the old days, Windows 8.1's help files are now stored on the Internet, so you'll need a connection to access them. Just open the Settings charm and choose Help to get started.

FURTHER READING

Ballew, Joli, *Configuring Windows 8.1*, Microsoft Press, 2014

Bott, Ed, *Introducing Windows 8.1 for IT Professionals*, Microsoft Press, 2013

Boyce, Jim *et al.*, *Windows 8.1 Bible*, John Wiley & Sons, 2014

Brockschmidt, Kraig, *Programming Windows® 8 Apps with HTML, CSS, and JavaScript*, Microsoft Press, 2012

McFedries, Paul, *PCs for Grown-ups: Getting the Most Out of Your Windows 8 Computer*, QUE, 2013

Miller, Michael, *Computer Basics Absolute Beginner's Guide, Windows 8.1 Edition*, QUE, 2014

Nathan, Adam, *Windows 8.1 Apps with XAML and C# Unleashed*, Sams, 2013

Northrup, Tony, *Windows 8.1 Inside Out*, Microsoft Press, 2013

Price, Michael, *Windows 8 for Seniors*, In Easy Steps, 2012

Rathbone, Andy, *Windows 8.1 for Dummies*, John Wiley & Sons, 2013

Sievers, Tim, *Top 100 Tips for Windows 8: Discover the Secrets of Windows 8*, CreateSpace Independent Publishing Platform, 2012

Smith, Stephie, *BASICS of Windows: The Easy Guide to Your PC*, CreateSpace Independent Publishing Platform, 2013

Stanek, William R., *Windows 8.1 Administration Pocket Consultant: Essentials & Configuration*, Microsoft Press, 2013

Williams, Andy, *Migrating to Windows 8: For computer users without a touch screen, coming from XP, Vista or Windows 7*, CreateSpace Independent Publishing Platform, 2013

Yarnold, Stuart, *Windows 8 Tips, Tricks & Shortcuts*, In Easy Steps, 2012

USEFUL WEBSITES

www.askvg.com/
This website coves tips, tweaks, troubleshooting
and customisation for Windows.

www.computerhope.com/cleaning.htm
Feel like your PC needs a spring clean?
This site gives lots of information and tips
on how to do so safely.

www.facebook.com/windowsmag
Facebook version of the Windows Magazine,
which posts interesting stories and news items
related to the world of computing.

www.howtogeek.com/
A site offering discussion, articles and
reviews on all things PC related.

www.itpro.co.uk/desktop-software
News and insight from the IT business.

www.nidirect.gov.uk/choosing-a-computer
Site offering straightforward advice on the
best type of computer to choose for your needs,
with links to other computer-related basics.

www.pcadvisor.co.uk
Great advice on all things PC: device
reviews, articles, forums and more.

www.recyclenow.com
If you are upgrading your computer, or any of
your hardware, this site will tell you what to do
with it – don't just throw it in the bin.

strongpasswordgenerator.com
Need a new password? This site will help
you choose a good one.

www.techspot.com
A great, general interest site for everything to do
with PCs, with reviews, downloads, forums and more.

which.co.uk/technology/computing
Head to this site for unbiased advice on buying
the computer and related technology that suits
you best.

windowsforum.com/
A useful forum which contains information on
how to deal with many common issues and
questions about Windows.

windows.microsoft.com/en-gb/windows/support
Go to this site for help and information on
anything Windows related.

winsupersite.com/
A great site covering all things Windows related.

INDEX